AQUARIUS

—SUN SIGN SERIES—

AQUARIUS

SUN SIGN SERIES
JOANNA MARTINE WOOLFOLK

TAYLOR TRADE PUBLISHING
LANHAM • NEW YORK • BOULDER • TORONTO • PLYMOUTH, UK

Published by Taylor Trade Publishing
An imprint of The Rowman & Littlefield Publishing Group, Inc.
4501 Forbes Boulevard, Suite 200, Lanham, Maryland 20706
www.rlpgtrade.com

Estover Road, Plymouth PL6 7PY, United Kingdom

Distributed by National Book Network

British Library Cataloguing in Publication Information Available

Library of Congress Cataloging-in-Publication Data

Woolfolk, Joanna Martine.
  Aquarius / Joanna Martine Woolfolk.
    p. cm.—(Sun sign series)
  ISBN 978-1-58979-563-1 (pbk. : alk. paper)—ISBN 978-1-58979-538-9 (electronic)
  1. Aquarius (Astrology) I. Title.
  BF1727.7.W66 2011
  133.5'276—dc23   2011018305

∞™ The paper used in this publication meets the minimum requirements of American
National Standard for Information Sciences—Permanence of Paper for Printed Library
Materials, ANSI/NISO Z39.48-1992.

Printed in the United States of America

I dedicate this book to the memory of
William Woolfolk
whose wisdom continues to guide me,

and to
James Sgandurra
who made everything bloom again.

CONTENTS

ABOUT THE AUTHOR

Astrologer Joanna Martine Woolfolk has had a long career as an author, columnist, lecturer, and counselor. She has written the monthly horoscope for numerous magazines in the United States, Europe, and Latin America—among them *Marie Claire*, *Harper's Bazaar*, *Redbook*, *Self*, *YM*, *House Beautiful*, and *StarScroll International*.

In addition to the best-selling *The Only Astrology Book You'll Ever Need*, Joanna is the author of *Sexual Astrology*, which has sold over a million copies worldwide, and *Astrology Source*, an interactive CD-ROM.

Joanna is a popular television and radio personality who has been interviewed by Barbara Walters, Regis Philbin, and Sally Jessy Raphael. She has appeared in a regular astrology segment on *New York Today* on NBC-TV and on *The Fairfield Exchange* on

CT Cable Channel 12, and she appears frequently on television and radio shows around the country. You can visit her website at www.joannamartinewoolfolk.com.

ACKNOWLEDGMENTS

Many people contribute to the creation of a book, some with ideas and editorial suggestions, and some unknowingly through their caring and love.

Among those who must know how much they helped is Jed Lyons, the elegant, erudite president of my publishers, the Rowman & Littlefield Publishing Group. Jed gave me the idea for this Sun Sign series, and I am grateful for his faith and encouragement.

Enormous gratitude also to Michael K. Dorr, my literary agent and dear friend, who has believed in me since we first met and continues to be my champion. I thank Michael for his sharp editor's eye and imbuing me with confidence.

Two people who don't know how much they give are my beloved sister and brother, Patricia G. Reynhout and Dr. John T. Galdamez. They sustain me with their unfailing devotion and support.

We are born at a given moment, in a given place, and like vintage years of wine, we have the qualities of the year and of the season in which we are born.

Carl Gustav Jung

INTRODUCTION

When my publishers suggested I write a book devoted solely to Aquarius, I was thrilled. I've long wanted to concentrate exclusively on your wonderful sign. You are very special in the zodiac. Astrology teaches that Aquarius is the sign of hope, friendship, and expansive ideas. Your sign represents originality and inventiveness, intellectual exploration, camaraderie and peacemaking, and the freedom to be unique. You have a curious mind and a caring heart, and you strive to create positive change. You're a visionary—Aquarius is the sign of the Awakener. Karmic teachers say you were picked to be Aquarius because of your heroic deeds in a previous life to help bring harmony to mankind. But whether or not one believes in past lives, in *this* life you are Aquarius, the remarkable sign of imagination, humaneness, and the passionate pursuit of knowledge.

These days it has become fashionable to be a bit dismissive of Sun signs (the sign that the Sun was in at the time of your birth). Some people sniff that "everyone knows about Sun signs." They say the descriptions are too cookie-cutter, too much a cardboard figure, too inclusive (how can every Aquarian be the same?).

Of course every Aquarian is not the same! And many of these differences not only are genetic and environmental, but are differences in your *charts*. Another Aquarian would not necessarily have your Moon sign, or Venus sign, or Ascendant. However, these are factors to consider later—after you have studied your Sun sign. (In *The Only Astrology Book You'll Ever Need*, I cover in depth differences in charts: different Planets, Houses, Ascendants, etc.)

First and foremost, you are an Aquarian. Aquarius is the sign the Sun was traveling through at the time of your birth.* The Sun is our most powerful planet. (In astrological terms, the Sun is referred to as a planet even though technically it is a "luminary.") It gives us life, warmth, energy, food. It is the force that sustains us on Earth. The Sun is also the most important and pervasive influence in your horoscope and in many ways determines how others see you. Your Sun sign governs your individuality, your distinctive style, and your drive to fulfill your goals.

Your sign of Aquarius symbolizes the role you are given to play in this life. It's as if at the moment of your birth you were pushed onstage into a drama called *This Is My Life*. In this drama, you are the starring actor—and Aquarius is the character you play. What aspects of this character are you going to project? The Aquarian intelligence, ingenuity, sense of brotherhood, and openness to the new? Its friendliness, kindness, deep loyalty, and commitment to truth? Or its rebelliousness, arrogance, eccentricity, iconoclasm, and emotional detachment? Your sign of Aquarius describes your journey through this life, for it is your task to evolve into a perfect Aquarian.

For each of us, the most interesting, most gripping subject is *self*. The longer I am an astrologer—which at this point is half my

---

*From our viewpoint here on Earth, the Sun travels around the Earth once each year. Within the space of that year, the Sun moves through all twelve signs of the zodiac, spending approximately one month in each sign.

lifetime—the more I realize that what we all want to know about is ourselves. "Who am I?" you ask. You want to know what makes you tick, why you have such intense feelings, and whether others are also insecure. People ask me questions like, "What kind of man should I look for?" "Why am I discontented with my job?" or "The man I'm dating is an Aries; will we be happy together?" They ask me if they'll ever find true love and when they will get out of a period of sadness or fear or the heavy burden of problems. They ask about their path in life and how they can find more fulfillment.

So I continue to see that the reason astrology exists is to answer questions about you. Basically, it's all about *you*. Astrology has been described as a stairway leading into your deeper self. It holds out the promise that you do not have to pass through life reacting blindly to experience, that you can within limits direct your own destiny and in the process reach a truer self-understanding.

Astrologically, the place to begin the study of yourself is your Sun Sign. In this book, you'll read about your many positive qualities as well as your Aquarius issues and negative inclinations. You'll find insights into your power and potentials, advice about love and sex, career guidance, health and diet tips, and information about myriads of objects, places, concepts, and things to which Aquarius is attached. You'll also find topics not usually included in other astrology books—such as how Aquarius fits in with Chinese astrology and with numerology.

Come with me on this exploration of the "infinite variety" (in Shakespeare's phrase) of being an Aquarius.

Joanna Martine Woolfolk
Stamford, Connecticut
June 2011

AQUARIUS

JANUARY 20–FEBRUARY 18

AQUARIUS, PISCIS AUSTRALIS & BALLON AEROSTATIQUE pl. 20.

PART ONE

ALL ABOUT YOU

ILLUMINATING QUOTATIONS

"Hell, there are no rules here; we're trying to accomplish something."

—Thomas A. Edison, inventor and scientist, an Aquarius

"I thought how unpleasant it is to be locked out, and then I thought how it is worse to be locked in."

—Virginia Woolf, author and essayist, an Aquarius

"I owned the world that hour as I rode over it. Free of the earth, free of the mountains, free of the clouds—but how inseparably I was bound to them."

—Charles Lindbergh, aviator (first to fly nonstop over the Atlantic Ocean), an Aquarius

"Nobody can be exactly like me. Even I have trouble doing it."

—Tallullah Bankhead, actress and *bonne vivante*, an Aquarius

"Everybody is an artist. Everybody is God. It's just that they're inhibited."

—Yoko Ono, artist, musician, and activist, an Aquarius

"So you know what I'm going to do? I'm going to do something really outrageous. I'm going to tell the truth."

—John Travolta, actor, an Aquarius

YOUR AQUARIUS PERSONALITY

YOUR MOST LIKEABLE TRAIT: Friendliness

The bright side of Aquarius: Brilliant thinker, idealistic, creative, tolerant, a humanitarian with a progressive outlook
The dark side of Aquarius: Contrariness, unpredictability, tactlessness, aloofness, fixed in opinion

Aquarius is the sign of rational thinking, humanitarianism, hopes, and ideals. You're drawn to ideas and inventions, and have a deep thirst for knowledge. You want to express totally the unique individual you are—to live a life of autonomy and harmony. To you a perfect world would be one in which people were free to develop their own potential. Yet in pursuing your own potential, you can be quirky, thorny, and iconoclastic—breaking rules and creating conflict just to be unconventional. You're also emotionally aloof; you want privacy and space. Curiously, these qualities coexist with your supreme friendliness and kindliness. You sincerely want to help your fellow human being and are gifted at inspiring groups to bring about positive change. At heart, you're an activist and rebel.

Astrologers are fond of this eleventh sign of the zodiac, for Aquarius is the sign of the future, of the visionary, some say of astrology itself. Aquarians are unorthodox, original people—sort of wacky, witty madcaps who refuse to follow the crowd and go their own way. You *like* being different. You not only march to a different drummer, you make up new music as you go along.

Intellectual independence is your most marked characteristic. You're a pioneer and a groundbreaker who high-steps your way through life, making grand plans and minting ideas no one else has thought of. In the sign of Aquarius, the combination of a Fixed quality (representing persistence) and an Air element (representing intellect and communication) under the influence of the planet of change, Uranus, creates a personality that is liberal, progressive, yet fixed in opinion.

Your inflexibility shows up when others least expect it (in keeping with your penchant for unconventionality). It may be in defense of an idea you have, a trip you've decided on, a habit you refuse to give up—whatever the cause, someone will suddenly come in conflict with your Aquarian obstinacy. You refuse to compromise or give an inch. You're a strange mix of an avant-garde thinker whose opinions are written in stone. You cheerfully ignore what others think and strike off on new paths, unbound by precedent, because there are so many more exciting things to discover that way. In tune with the far-out and daring, you think boredom is a communicable disease and take every opportunity to avoid it.

Your character is a system of paradoxes. You enjoy being with people but are content to be alone. You like travel but love relaxing at home. You are friendly and outgoing but also detached and reserved. You have both a scientific and an artistic turn of mind. In a career, you often are involved in two distinct areas of work.

Your astrological symbol is the Water Bearer—often Aquarius is mistaken for a Water sign. Aquarius is an *Air* sign. You are a communicator, an idea person. People born under this sign live most intensely in their minds. The "water" being poured out by the Water Bearer stands for truth. You are a truth teller; you give out opinions and observations. You dispense wisdom. You are a seeker of knowledge, rational, open-minded, gifted with breadth of vision. Chock full of information, you still search for more. You always want to know what lies on the other side of the mountain. One Aquarian recently declared, "It annoys me to find out there's something out there I've never heard of. I need to know what it is!"

You can be objective in judgment, for you don't let emotion get in the way. This appears to give you the ability to stand outside yourself, to rise above ordinary human frailty. Your built-in distrust of emotion compels you to struggle against its chains, and this may become a source of inner conflict.

Problems arise when your sense of identity becomes inextricably linked to your ideas. Like Gemini, another Air sign, you have a lot of ego invested in your opinions. Your great weakness is a tendency to inflate the importance of your thinking—and to pose as an expert on any subject. When others disagree, you take this as an attack on your personhood. Your fixity turns into willfulness and rebelliousness for the sake of being a rebel. You deliberately refuse to recognize that your idea isn't working in the real world of your relationships or career—and you sabotage yourself by insisting on your way even if your way proves to be unfeasible.

You are very people-oriented, addicted to the study of human beings, and an inveterate people watcher. You're extraordinarily intuitive—out of the blue you seem to get flashes of insight into human beings and their motives. You're outgoing and amiable, and you crackle with vitality; you attract friends wherever you go. Witty, articulate, and a fascinating conversationalist, you usually can find an imaginative way of expressing yourself. Indeed, you have a talent for making people laugh with a pithy phrase that sums up a situation—though those who tangle with you quickly discover how your sharp verbal skills can deflate pomposity and pretension.

You possess a true common touch yet never lose your own strong individuality. Whomever you meet, you remain you—that amusing, inquisitive, interested person who wants to know what makes others tick. Your gift is for dealing with all kinds of personalities from every walk of life, no matter what their station or status. You never put on airs, nor are you cowed by anyone's wealth or position. If you met the queen of England, you would be your natural self.

We're all related, you believe, because we're all human beings. You are genuinely interested in why a person thinks this way or that. The nicest part is that you do not judge. You willingly grant to others what you consider an inalienable right—the freedom to be unique. For you, the ultimate liberation is simply the freedom to be oneself.

As a student of human behavior, you have great tolerance for the weaknesses and foibles to which all mankind is heir. You are a humanitarian, concerned with the welfare of the world, but do not get deeply involved in intimate relationships. There is always a certain distant quality to you, a detachment or aloofness of spirit. You seem to disassociate yourself from emotion.

However, the cool, arm's-length impression you give can be deceiving. In the zodiac, Aquarius symbolizes friendship, and you can form close and enduring ties. Beneath your detached exterior beats a stubbornly loyal heart. No one is a truer, finer friend than Aquarius. Completely free of malice, you'll do anything to be helpful. Yet you'll never let the other person become dependent on you. Your affection comes with no strings attached.

Because independence is your way of life, you will sacrifice even a close personal relationship in order to maintain it. Trying to fence you in or tie you down won't work. If you feel trapped, you try to break free at any cost. Your sign of Aquarius also represents future hopes and yearnings, and for you, what's over is done with. Even the present is often left behind. As for the past, you just want to escape it and, like Peter Pan, head straight on to morning. You're wonderful at hatching schemes and dreams, plotting trips, setting goals. The unusual—in people, places, and projects—is what really interests you.

You are not a narrow, petty person; you're an idealist who wants nothing more than for everyone to be happy in a harmonious world. You're concerned with greater goals—your ambition is to do something important and meaningful. Many Aquarians go into politics or become involved in social causes. This is the astrological sign of hopes and wishes, and you are the kind who follows a dream. History is dotted with progressive Aquarian thinkers such as Charles Darwin, Abraham Lincoln, Susan B. Anthony, Thomas Edison, and Franklin Delano Roosevelt.

An Aquarian will hatch up a grandiose scheme for improving the way things are, but your main interest is in creating the idea, not translating it into action through work. Hard work doesn't interest you. You are creative, imaginative, endlessly willing to experiment, but the drudgery of detail and the minutiae of management are not your style.

You'd rather invent a new utopian scheme and let others grapple with the hard realities. In fact, you truly don't want to deal with reality at all. Life should be ideal, and you often refuse to accept that the world doesn't work on your ideals. Neither are you practical or down-to-earth. You're lost in the clouds, and it irks you terribly to have to learn to grapple with *what is*. You can be a stubborn child who says, "I want to do exactly what I want—when I want to!"

The Aquarian life lesson is it's not enough to be brilliant. You need to make something of your brilliance and be willing to be grounded and to compromise. You are so determined not to be like anyone else that you are sometimes contrary just to be different. You have the least regard for convention of any zodiacal sign, which often gives you a reputation for being eccentric. Just as you are broad-minded about the faults of others, you take for granted that your shortcomings will be overlooked.

Sometimes you will be argumentative not because you feel deeply, but simply because you enjoy the intellectual exercise. You are quickly bored and take delight in verbally provoking anyone you consider stodgy and dull.

Nevertheless, Aquarians are among the kindest people in the world, treasured for the optimism and cheer you give out to others. Easygoing, reasonable, slow to take offense, never mean-hearted, you believe in live-and-let-live. Honest, helpful, altruistic, and best of all never boring, you can change anyone's life for the better just by becoming part of it.

THE INNER YOU

The most frequent question you ask is "Why?" You want to understand what makes other people tick. Their lives fascinate you because you hope they will offer you insights into your own. You have plenty of love to give, and you want nothing more than to have lots of interesting friends, a wonderful love relationship, fulfilling work, and for the world to be a better place and everyone to be happy. Not much to ask, is it? One of your best-kept secrets is how shy and insecure you are. You wonder if the people you care about feel the same way about you—this is why you work so hard to make others like you. You want to share yourself but are afraid of losing who you are or becoming what other people think you should be. Yet somehow your feelings of insecurity manage to coexist with a belief that you are someone special.

HOW OTHERS SEE YOU

You're often regarded as slightly eccentric—not necessarily *strange*, but certainly an independent character, a kind of daredevil with an unusual way of looking at things. People consider you a pathfinder, a member of the real avant-garde. They think you have a wicked sense of humor, an ability to shock and amuse at the same time. They know you're open to new ideas, especially when those ideas are yours. People are drawn to your friendliness and enthusiasm, but they withdraw quickly when you turn acid-tongued. Sometimes, because you need so much personal freedom, you give the impression of being uncaring or distant. Those around you may also become annoyed at your stubbornness.

GUARD AGAINST: Being Different for the Sake of Being Different

It's in your Aquarian nature to want to choose your own course and take orders from no one. You're an individual who stands out from the crowd. But keep in mind that, in general, people look with disfavor on those who deviate from what everyone else is doing and saying. The one who doesn't fit into accepted modes tends to be ostracized. The underlying reason is an atavistic fear; the tribe says, "If you're not one of us, then you're an enemy." We no longer live in tribes, but we do live in an interdependent society—and you need to have grace to hold your own without stirring up resentment.

Aquarius takes pride in being unconventional, and you're prone toward tipping into the eccentric side of the behavior scale. Also, you have a tendency to put forward opinions as "truth" (this is what you believe, so it must be true). You can be heedless about what you say to whom. Often your *outré* behaviors will put obstacles in your path to a goal, especially a goal in which you need others.

One of your lessons is to learn how to manage your Aquarian genius-quality so you don't arouse ill feeling. Actually, you have a wonderful tool—your *friendliness*. You enjoy group associations in which there's give-and-take and mutual support. You tend not to be on guard with people, and you don't harbor secret resentment. Therefore, to create a balance between being a unique genius and a success within a group, work on your strengths (responsiveness, sociability, openness to the exchange of ideas). You want space to do your own thing, but you don't want to feel eternally misunderstood, and you certainly don't want to be exiled.

You need an environment that gives you autonomy *and* you need harmonious relationships with colleagues and associates. If you strive too hard to be different, you're likely to defeat the purpose of being independent.

YOUR GREATEST CHALLENGE: To Open Your Heart

You need to learn how to bridge the cool distance you put between yourself and another, and make genuine connection. As an Air sign, you live in your head. Feelings are routed through your mind; then you think about them, examine them, and try to filter out what's uncomfortable. Additionally, Aquarius isn't wired for closeness. Being extremely independent, you fiercely maintain your space. You don't want others intruding, telling you what to do, how to live. You set yourself apart to emphasize your own qualities. People's emotional demands make you feel claustrophobic.

All this leads to separateness between you and others—which, curiously, coexists with the fact you're caring, generous, and giving. You have humanitarian instincts; you would never say no to someone in need. You're a wonderful friend, for in this relationship you can give advice, sympathy, and practical assistance. Yet these gifts tend not to be emotional, per se. They come out of your ability to assess situations calmly and logically, and offer what's needed at the right time.

Your challenge is to connect on a *heart* level. And a real key to doing this is to use what you're already superlative at—communicating. Open yourself to conversation, an exchange of what's on your mind. When you talk, the flow of your ideas leads to your talking about what you're *thinking* about your feelings, and in time this becomes a flow of feelings. As rapport develops, so does closeness. Soon it becomes easier to let your true emotions rise to the surface. You will trust your intuition. You'll be able to weed out shallow alliances and move deeper into meaningful relationships that sustain you (in family, friendship). Ultimately, you will be in balance between head and heart.

YOUR ALTER EGO

Astrology gives us many tools in our lives to help manage our struggles and solve problems. One of these tools is to reach into your opposite sign in the zodiac—your polarity. For you, Aquarius, this is Leo, sign of power and pride, vitality and creativity. Leo is dramatic, fiery, filled with enthusiasm—and inherent in its character is the need to be *involved*. Spontaneous and full of zest, Leo leaps with passion into whatever seizes its attention.

Leo is the sign that symbolizes life in its fullest bloom. Its ruler, the Sun, has dominion over the power to develop one's own being. In this regard, you and Leo are much alike. Aquarius and Leo are both motivated by a drive to express their identity. (Astrology describes this as the "journey of a hero.") The difference, though, is Leo concentrates on expanding its ego, whereas Aquarius focuses on expanding its consciousness.

This means that Leo, who needs to be the center of its universe, embraces others and tries to make them part of itself. Anything Leo becomes involved in (a job, lover, new project) Leo sees as an extension of itself. The fervor and magnanimity of this sign reaches out to *include*. Leo operates very much in the now and lives through its feelings.

You, Aquarius, can benefit from adopting some of Leo's ability to connect. Aquarius loves humanity though not necessarily human beings. Of course, this is an exaggeration—you're utterly devoted to those to whom you do give your caring. But in general you want lots of space around you to engage in your varied interests and pursue your goals. You don't want to be suffocated by clingy relationships and dependent people. The big problem is that your cool, detached attitude can isolate you. Others withdraw from you, which can hurt. Like anyone, you want to be loved and admired—and you'll find that people are far more accessible to you if you incorporate a little of Leo's warm openheartedness.

In turn, Leo has many lessons to learn from you. In particular, Leo could make life work much more smoothly by espousing your philosophy of live and let live. Leo insists that others follow its lead—it wants to be monarch and struggles for supremacy. Leo can be overbearing, and its constant need for attention is very trying. Aquarius knows how to step away and not become embroiled in ego battles. You allow others the freedom you insist for yourself—and you certainly don't want to be surrounded by sycophants and slaves. At your core, you want a peaceable existence. You're a caring idealist who can be counted on to do the right thing. It would be a safe, harmonious, and happy world if all of humanity could emulate you.

AQUARIUS IN LOVE

You are charming, funny, and brainy, and you don't have to play games to fascinate. You play yourself. Aquarius has a special magnetism that some astrologers call "distant glamour." Like all the Air signs (Gemini, Libra, Aquarius), you live in a world of ideas and possess a certain detached quality. This is very tantalizing—it attracts those who want to stir your emotions.

However, in any romantic encounter your first contact has to be made through the mind. Before you can become physically stimulated, you must be intellectually stimulated. For Aquarius, the meeting of minds always precedes the meeting of bodies. You want to make love to *somebody*, not just *any*body.

You are not cold or removed from feeling, but warm and outgoing, concerned with others, and you do have a strong romantic streak. But for Aquarius, romance is an idea, an ideal, not a sweeping passion. Communication is what is important. You see a lover as an individual first and a bed partner second.

Certainly, in keeping with your unpredictability, you have an imaginative approach to sex. Your boudoir behavior is innovative and creative, and more than heavy-breathing passion, you seek novelty and diversion.

Still, you're not interested in sex for the sake of sex. If you're an Aquarius woman, a would-be lover has to convince you that you're not simply his target for tonight. He cannot make the mistake of treating you as a sex object. You expect to be courted, and a man should not press matters to a conclusion until he knows more about you than your telephone number. If you're an Aquarius man, you need to feel that your sexual partner also appreciates your brilliance and partakes of your passions of the mind.

In addition, with Aquarius's strong streak of independence, both male and female refuse to be fettered by binding demands. You cannot bear possessiveness or jealousy, and won't be dictated to by anyone's whims. The quickest way someone can lose you is to try to hold you fast. What intrigues you is the hill beyond the unexplored horizon; there's so much out there waiting to be discovered. Your romantic partner has to share your love of a challenge or he or she will soon be left behind. You will move on without a backward glance, a grand ship sailing on without an inkling of the tragedy in your wake.

Aquarius enjoys falling in love—you think this is a natural and delightful condition. But falling in love and loving mean two different things, and the latter is likely to bring out inner conflicts. Aquarius is a cerebral sign, and you're somewhat unnerved and embarrassed by emotion—and wary of it. It can be troublesome and tiresome.

Also, love represents a demand. Loving means making room for another person, and in common with the other Fixed signs (Taurus, Leo, and Scorpio), Aquarius does not adapt easily to others. Others have to adapt to *you*.

In general, in relationships (even in friendships) you're like a one-way mirror. You're able to see outward through this mirror, and observe and analyze, but others look back at a reflective surface. In a romantic relationship, this is a kiss of death because true love cannot develop. True intimacy can only happen with a two-way mirror.

Yet the Aquarian psyche is complicated by a fear of intimacy—of psychological exposure and vulnerability. You try various avenues of escape: work, study, social involvement, love of animals, multiple relationships.

In addition, when you're in any relationship, you have a nagging sense of "is this all there is?" You want something more and aren't sure what this is. (Something deeper? Something freer?) For Aquarius, a love relationship is problematical because you crave emotional and sexual intimacy, yet need great personal freedom, and you need to respect your lover as a friend. What often happens is you choose a partner who is interesting or intellectually powerful, but not perfect, and then go about creating distance between you.

The irony is that Aquarius is particularly good at giving. Showing your love in deeds comes naturally—you make your affection visible by helping and nurturing. Your astrological symbol, the Water Bearer, confirms this: It is a picture of Aquarius dispensing gifts to those in need.

And once you open your heart and your passions are directed toward a specific person, you are loyal and devoted. Lies and deceit are anathema—to you there can be no love without loyalty. When you make a promise, you stand by your word. After all, that is what honor and idealism are about, and those are hallmarks of your sign.

Indeed, some say Aquarius is the perfect mate because you're easy to deal with—tolerant, slow to take offense, never jealous or unreasonable, never overemotional or clinging. You try never to encroach on your lover's rights; you're willing to grant the same space and freedom you ask for yourself. You don't give orders or set rules and limits on a relationship. All you ask is for a lover to respect your privacy and not stand in the way of your far-reaching interests.

You want a companion for the journey ahead, and with you a love relationship has many of the elements of friendship—intellectual interests and social compatibility. You're a blend of friend, lover, sensualist, and adventurer.

TIPS FOR THOSE WHO WANT TO ATTRACT AQUARIUS

These highly social creatures make friends easily. They are amusing, interesting conversationalists who nonetheless prefer to discuss what is significant or important. Don't be surprised if they don't reach any conclusions, though. When you're dealing with eternal verities, it's hard to come to the point.

Aquarians are usually courteous but elusive. There is no way to breach this demeanor, especially not with a direct attack. When faced with a head-on approach, Aquarians tend to retreat.

It is easy to draw out their compassionate qualities. They are humanitarians whose interests stretch far beyond the horizon. They see the big picture, not its little flaws.

They are interested in books, art, or scientific matters. Most Aquarians have an interest in science. They are also fascinated by hobbies and gadgets. If you can't share all their interests, at least try not to be jealous of the fact Aquarians have so many. They can't help it; it's in their stars.

Aquarians are not steak and potatoes people; they prefer to try the little place that features *Chinois* cuisine—a combination of Chinese and continental cooking. Aquarians are always delighted with the different. By joining their spirit of exploration, you'll find no more stimulating companion in the zodiac.

Give them time to get to know you, trust you, and depend on you. Aquarians may take advice but are too smart to be fooled. They won't keep taking bad advice; they'll just avoid the adviser.

Never nag Aquarians about a mistake. They will acknowledge one readily enough, but then forget it. A mistake seems genuinely unimportant to them, and if you keep harping on it, they'll just think you are strange.

Important: Don't fence them in! Once they're in love with you, they'll stay pretty much in their pasture. But they must feel the escape routes are open.

AQUARIUS'S EROGENOUS ZONES: Tips for Those with an Aquarius Lover

Our bodies are very sensitive to the touch of another human being. The special language of touching is understood on a level more basic than speech. Each sign is linked to certain zones and areas of the body that are especially receptive and can receive sexual message through touch. Many books and manuals have been written about lovemaking, but few pay attention to the unique knowledge of erogenous zones supplied by astrology. You can use astrology to become a better, more sensitive lover.

The special erotic area for Aquarius is the calves and ankles. Touching, rubbing, fondling, or kissing this part of the anatomy will significantly arouse Aquarius's sexual desire.

Absentmindedly caress the ankle, moving up to the calf, and see how quickly Aquarius responds. Aquarians love having their lower legs and ankles laved with a sponge while reclining in a bath.

As a preliminary move to lovemaking, give Aquarius an erotic massage. Use your fingertips or fingernails, and stroke ever so gently. Begin at the ankles, and slowly describe circles around the anklebone. Make long strokes up the calves until you reach the knees. The area in back of the calves is particularly sensitive.

While making love, any position that allows contact with the calf and the ankle will increase Aquarius's sexual satisfaction.

AQUARIUS'S AMOROUS COMBINATIONS: YOUR LOVE PARTNERS

AQUARIUS AND ARIES

You'll enjoy plenty of fun and frolicking and never bore each other. Sexually, you two immediately discover a special erotic magic because Aries's passion inspires your originality. Actually, in all areas, your Aquarian imaginativeness meshes well with Aries's forcefulness—in bed, in business, socially, and as fellow adventurers. Also, each understands the other's need for freedom and outside interests and won't try to tie the other down. Professionally, you spark each other with new ideas, and as communicators you share humor and an interest in the world at large. However, neither of you likes to be dominated, and Aries *must* take the lead. Also, you tend to be irked by Aries self-centeredness—and Aries often thinks you're too stubborn. But if you two can work out these problems, the track ahead is clear as far as anyone can see.

AQUARIUS AND TAURUS

The two of you are drawn by curiosity about each other and, early on, by combustible sex. But you, Aquarius, are outgoing, friendly, laid-back emotionally, while Taurus is close, cuddly, and jealous. Your careless attitude toward love will baffle and finally enrage highly passionate Taurus, who doesn't want someone just to play with. Taurus's possessiveness makes you feel cornered and eager to pack a suitcase and go. You love to wander anywhere, while Taurus loves home. Aquarius and Taurus are both Fixed signs and both of you are stubborn—but in very different ways. You refuse to be conventional, while Taurus rigidly adheres to the values of family and security. Taurus is too staid for you, and you're too avant-garde for Taurus. Aquarius is interested in humane concerns; Taurus is single-minded about itself and its possessions. And so on and on and on.

AQUARIUS AND GEMINI

Gemini is willing to go along with your taste for experiment. In addition, you calm down Gemini's flightiness and are a stabilizing influence. You enjoy each other's quick, intelligent minds and will have scintillating conversations about people, ideas, and places. Both of you desire harmony and companionship with not a lot of emotional *Sturm und Drang*. As a couple, you love to socialize and have a wide range of outside activities, and neither of you is particularly jealous or proprietary. It's true that in certain ways you're an over-the-top pairing because Aquarius and Gemini both have a maverick quality and neither is going to hold the other in check. But generally the two of you just want to live and let live. You'll be fine bedmates and fascinating friends—and even if, in time, the relationship becomes platonic, you are beautifully attuned companions.

AQUARIUS AND CANCER

Aquarius hates Cancer's clinging restrictiveness and complaining, which stem from its constant need for proofs of love. You bristle at Cancer's possessiveness and feel swamped by its emotionalism. You're convivial and free with affection and can't understand why Cancer won't hang loose—and this makes sensitive Cancer feel even more neglected and rejected. Cancer wants a safe, secure home, but you need a very flexible living arrangement. You like space around you, which Cancer tries to close off. In essence, each of you represents what the other dislikes and fears. At the beginning, you were warmed by Cancer's inviting softness, and Cancer was lightened by your cheer. But almost immediately fondness grows cold. Vast differences keep widening the distance between you. Cancer most likely will want you to stay, but you're soon inclined to wander away.

AQUARIUS AND LEO

At first you each seem to have what the other admires—you have the sparkle and adventurism that Leo loves, and Leo's audacity enchants you. A great plus is Leo's delight in your sexual inventiveness, just as you are drawn to Leo's fire and robust zest. You two are opposites in the zodiac who start out on a grand high note—but then the notes go sour. Basically, Leo is physical and Aquarius is mental. Leo can't get from you the cooperation or the admiration it requires, and you resent Leo's attempt to rule. Both of you are Fixed signs, so both are stubborn—but unfortunately each thinks the other will adapt, which is never going to happen. You two also have different views of independence: to Aquarius it means freedom to explore new horizons; to Leo it means pursuing a glamorous, extravagant lifestyle. Aquarius is interested in the world; Leo is strictly interested in Leo.

AQUARIUS AND VIRGO

Aquarius and Virgo are mental signs rather than emotional, and when you first meet your minds click. Both of you are communicative and fascinated by new information, and both are service-oriented. But Virgo looks on the darker side of life while you are imaginative and optimistic. Very soon you feel hemmed in by Virgo's precise pickiness and its boundaries. You need activity, social events, a wide circle of acquaintances. Virgo enjoys a quiet existence with a few close friends. The goals of Aquarius and Virgo are very different: Aquarius wants to be as brilliant as possible; Virgo wants to be as efficient as possible. A big problem is Virgo needs someone with more warmth and sympathy, and you need someone more reckless and less shipshape. You two are intellectually compatible but unlikely to celebrate many anniversaries.

AQUARIUS AND LIBRA

Aquarius and Libra are Air signs who live in their heads and love to communicate. Immediately you're a harmonious pair with much in common, especially a creative outlook. Certainly warm, sensual Libra adores your romantic inventiveness and enthusiastically joins in your erotic fun and games. Also, diplomatic Libra knows just how to get around your quirky stubborn streak. You two like the way each other's minds work and share interests in music, theater, and the arts. Both of you love parties and other people and have numerous projects in common. There won't be arguments about who leads and who follows because you're both egalitarians. A fly in the ointment might be Libra's vain self-centeredness, but you're able to detach from this. You two should enjoy a lovely affair. However, for the long term, *someone* will have to settle down.

AQUARIUS AND SCORPIO

Aquarius can be airily detached, but when you connect with Scorpio, your affair begins intensely. Fueled by Scorpio's volatility and your Aquarian imaginativeness, sex is quite out of the ordinary. Regrettably, this burns out quickly. You're turned off by Scorpio's powerful and jealous passion, and Scorpio is upset by your unpredictable moods. Aquarius is looking for a companion in adventure, whereas Scorpio wants a committed consort. Aquarius needs space and distance and is aloof, unemotional, and restless. Scorpio is demanding, critical, and fiercely possessive; it needs to be closely intertwined. Aquarius and Scorpio are both Fixed signs, and both are entrenched—Scorpio in its murky depths and you in your individualism. When you start looking for happiness outside the home, you might as well keep right on traveling.

AQUARIUS AND SAGITTARIUS

A fun and zany match, for you bring out the madcap in each other. You two are so innovative about lovemaking you ought to charge admission. In addition, you inspire each other intellectually, for Aquarius has far-out, inventive ideas and Sagittarius is optimistic and visionary. You, Aquarius, can be dogmatic in your libertarian views, but this doesn't bother live-and-let-live Sagittarius. Both of you are highly social, fun-loving creatures who like people, seeing new places, and whatever is unpredictable. Sagittarius is charmed by all your interests, and you are buoyed by Sagittarius's enthusiasm. Basically, you're unconventional companions who make each other happy. You also give each other the long rein each needs—and the best part is neither of you is jealous when the other isn't home.

AQUARIUS AND CAPRICORN

Aquarius and Capricorn both have a strong sense of self, and you attract each other because of your intelligences. You're also drawn into early sexual passion that soon fizzles away. The basic problem is you want to be free and Capricorn wants to dominate. You have a great many opinions about everything and welcome neither advice nor orders from rigid Capricorn. You're continually on the go and like to spend money. Capricorn considers this frivolous and tries to impose strict controls. Capricorn is cautious, solid, and straightforward, and doesn't understand your adventurous ideas. You will view Capricorn as narrow and blinkered, and Capricorn will see you as eccentric and a social embarrassment. Though you're both stubborn enough to try to hang in, long-term prospects are bleak. A brief rapport at best before boredom sets in and damps the fire.

AQUARIUS AND AQUARIUS

Some same-sign matches don't work because they're too much alike. But the pairing of Aquarius and Aquarius brings out your positives of idealism and adventurism, and downplays negatives (such as rebelliousness). You admire and like each other and especially enjoy each other's sense of humor. Inventive, progressive, attracted to the new and unusual, you two are wonderfully suited sexually and share wide-ranging interests. Each of you is involved in all kinds of projects and friendships. With so many outside activities going, you're likely to be apart as much as you are together. This is fine with you two—just take care you don't find yourselves drifting too far apart. Aquarius is a stubborn sign, but you two agree on most things and both of you are much more rational than emotional. Your love won't be as deep as a well, but it will draw water.

AQUARIUS AND PISCES

You are intrigued by Pisces's romantic charm, and Pisces is drawn to your visionary outlook. Sensual, imaginative Pisces will go along with anything you want, and you two achieve an unusual sexual intimacy. You also have in common an idealistic view; you both envision a better world and rosier future. However, you two are so different you're soon traveling in separate directions. You're future oriented; Pisces dwells in the past. You filter the world through your mind; Pisces is subjective about everything. Pisces is dependent, indecisive, vague, and timid, and needs someone strong to take control. You shun any kind of demands and hate those swampy Pisces emotions. Things truly unravel as Pisces insists on more and more testaments of love. When you feel hemmed in by that all-enveloping Piscean web, you will struggle free and go your own way.

YOUR AQUARIUS CAREER PATH

Aquarius is the sign of hopes, wishes, and dreams, which perfectly describes your bent in a career. You're drawn to the dream, what lies beyond the horizon, the thing that hasn't been done yet. Money is fine if it comes along, but you're far less interested in financial power than in exploring something that enthralls you.

You're wretched if you have to work under other people's rules, or even with others looking over your shoulder. Because you're a free spirit and very independent, you do best freelancing, self-employed, owning your own business, or running a special department of your own. You can be a hard worker, but not a routinized one. Anything that smacks of the humdrum, boring, and repetitive is anathema. From the start, you tend to follow one of two paths: You enter an ordinary profession and turn it into something highly unique, or you immediately leap off the beaten track and keep on going to a farther realm.

Actually, you do attract wealth because your innovative ideas can be very profitable. But to you, success means the mental gratification of breakthroughs and the unfolding of the new. Basically, you're an inventor who sees the world differently from others—and if you can wake up in the morning and look forward to discovery in your work, you're in your perfect element.

An individualist and an innovator, your great talent is seeing what's possible and matching this with the energy to put a plan into motion. Also, you approach problems with an unbiased mind that looks beyond "good" and "bad" to what *is*—and then you begin inventing a solution.

Another career advantage is your skill for working with and blending into a group. You have a magnetic ability to relate to all kinds of personalities. People feel comfortable with you. You sway others to your point of view, galvanize them to take action. You have *charisma*.

With your amazing brainpower, you can be successful at almost anything you put your mind to. Your humanitarian instincts draw you toward politics (especially political reform), law, and social work. You're at home with technology, machines, and gadgets, and the world of computer technology and programming is wide open to you. You'd make a good inventor or scientist in such fields as astronomy, astrophysics, aviation, and space research. Indeed, any kind of research is your métier, for you're focused on digging out the truth. Medicine, psychiatry, and psychology suit your brilliance. Architecture and engineering utilize your skill for envisioning. And because you speak and write well, you can make your mark as an author or in the entertainment world.

Everyone, of course, needs to find work that expresses who he or she is, but for Aquarius this is particularly important and particularly hard to find. You need work that combines *integrity* with igniting your curiosity—but because the world can be venal, much of the time Aquarius feels like a stranger in a strange land.

Another difficulty is you're unrealistic about how much you can accomplish and tend to promise more than you can deliver. This exacts a toll as you become increasingly stressed because you're not living up to your word. In addition, you have a way of shutting out what you don't want to hear, for example, another person's suggestion for a better way of handling something. You become fixed in your opinions and turn a deaf ear to anyone else's—and your fixity becomes rigidity. The huge difference between perseverance and stubbornness is that the former shows forward movement and the latter is staying stuck in doing things one way—*your* way. You feel you sacrifice a great deal to your ideals and can't understand why you don't receive cooperation. It's likely that your undiplomatic approach ("I'll do it *my* way, period!") alienates those who could assist you.

Still, you are supremely gifted, and when you can find the balance between visionary dreams and hard reality, between originality and practicality, you are lit with the power to do long-remembered work and make far-reaching changes in this world.

AQUARIUS AND HEALTH: ADVICE FROM ASTROLOGY

Your well-being depends on managing your hyperactive nervous system. Because your mind runs at high frequency, you tend to suffer from insomnia. You overtax yourself physically and work to exhaustion. You're so used to living with mental tension, you're often unaware when this has become a state of unrelieved stress. A culprit is the fact you focus on mind activities rather than looking after your body. You're lax about exercising and eating nutritiously, which are the keys to your good health. Exercise should be the calming kind (no overexertion). Yoga, brisk walks, swimming, and dancing yield huge benefits. You tend to suffer from muscle cramps, and regular body movement relieves this. A balanced diet low in salt, fat, and cholesterol keeps blood pressure at healthy levels and gives you proper fuel to lead your busy, active life.

Advice and useful tips about health are among the most important kinds of information that astrology provides. Health and well-being are of paramount concern to human beings. Love, money, or career takes second place, for without good health we cannot enjoy anything in life.

Astrology and medicine have had a long marriage. Hippocrates (born around 460 B.C.), the Greek philosopher and physician who is considered the father of medicine, said, "A physician without a knowledge of astrology has no right to call himself a physician." Indeed, up until the eighteenth century, the study of astrology and its relationship to the body was very much a part of a doctor's training. When a patient became ill, a chart was immediately drawn up. This guided the doctor in both diagnosis and treatment, for the chart would tell when the crisis would come and what medicine would help. Of course, modern Western doctors no longer use astrology to treat illness. However, astrology can still be a useful tool in helping to understand and maintain our physical well-being.

THE PART OF THE BODY RULED BY AQUARIUS

Each sign of the zodiac governs a specific part of the body. These associations date back to the beginning of astrology. Curiously, the part of the body that a sign rules is in some ways the strongest and in other ways the weakest area for natives of that sign.

Your sign of Aquarius rules the circulatory system and the shins, calves, and ankles. The lower leg represents active locomotion, and Aquarians are characterized as progressive and forward thinking. You're generally strong and healthy, with good coordination, well-shaped legs, and slender ankles. You tend to be very active mentally, more than you are physically, and you have a slight tendency to put on weight if you're not careful. Often your health will take an unexpected sudden turn for the worse, and just as quickly reverse again. Your illnesses come on without apparent reason.

The lower part of the legs and ankles is an area very susceptible for Aquarius. At times, your ankles swell and cause problems. You are prone to varicose veins and cramps in the lower legs. Accidents, cuts, bruises, sprains, and fractures are suffered more frequently on the shins, calves, and ankles than on other parts of the body. Aquarians suffer circulatory problems, hardening of the arteries, anemia, and low blood pressure. Cold weather is particularly hard on you, and you're prone to frostbite.

Uranus, Aquarius's ruling planet, governs the circulatory system and the pineal gland. The pineal gland, found at the base of the skull, produces melatonin, the hormone that regulates the sleep/wake pattern in the human body. The ancients called this gland the "seat of the soul" and thought it was what remained of man's "third eye." The sign of Aquarius is associated with the concept of unusual and mystical knowledge.

DIET AND HEALTH TIPS FOR AQUARIUS

You need a healthy diet to maintain vitality and to keep your weight at the perfect level. You tend to immerse yourself in projects and activities, and this leaves little time for balanced meals. As an inveterate snacker, you often eat the wrong things while on the run.

Aquarius's cell salt* is sodium chloride, which is common table salt. This does not mean, however, that you should heavily salt the food you eat (quite the opposite!). This will only lead to bloating,

---

* *Cell salts* (also known as *tissue salts*) are mineral compounds found in human tissue cells. These minerals are the only substances our cells cannot produce by themselves. The life of cells is relatively short, and the creation of new cells depends on the presence of these minerals.

kidney disorders, hardening of the arteries, and problems with sluggish circulation. On the other hand, lack of sodium chloride in the body results in dehydration. You need to absorb sodium chloride naturally, by eating the right foods. These include ocean fish, lobster, tuna, clams, oysters, spinach, radishes, celery, cabbage, lettuce, corn, romaine, squash, lentils, almonds, pecans, walnuts, apples, peaches, pears, lemons, and oranges. You should follow a diet that limits fattening foods and is high in protein, fresh fruits and vegetables, and whole-grain breads. Fruits high in vitamin C will keep the veins in your legs healthy. Other foods that are very good for you are chicken, veal, beets, broccoli, carrots, peppers, tomatoes, strawberries, pineapple, pomegranates, figs, dates, brown rice, buckwheat, whole wheat, yogurt, and natural cheeses.

Fresh air and exercise are very important in order to relieve tension and rev up energy. You should take great care, however, when doing anything that might injure the calves and ankles. Brisk walks are excellent, for they get circulation going in the legs. You should not run, even when in a hurry, for you're likely to trip and fall. Puffiness in the legs and ankles can be counteracted by elevating the legs, and an afternoon nap keeps up vitality. You should cut down on caffeine, which makes you nervous.

Aquarians are apt to get gray hair fairly early in life—but you should not worry that this means the onset of premature old age!

THE DECANATES AND CUSPS OF AQUARIUS

Decanate and *cusp* are astrological terms that subdivide your Sun sign. These subdivisions further define and emphasize certain qualities and character traits of your Sun sign, Aquarius.

WHAT IS A DECANATE?

Each astrological sign is divided into three parts, and each part is called a *decanate* or a *decan* (the terms are used interchangeably).

The word comes from the Greek word *dekanoi*, meaning "ten days apart." The Greeks took their word from the Egyptians, who divided their year into 360 days.* The Egyptian year had twelve months of thirty days each, and each month was further divided into three sections of ten days each. It was these ten-day sections the Greeks called *dekanoi*.

*The Egyptians soon found out that a 360-day year was inaccurate and so added on five extra days. These were feast days and holidays, and not counted as real days.

Astrology still divides the zodiac into decanates. There are twelve signs in the zodiac, and each sign is divided into three decanates. You might picture each decanate as a room. You were born in the sign of Aquarius, which consists of three rooms (decanates). In which room of Aquarius were you born?

The zodiac is a 360-degree circle. Each decanate is ten degrees of that circle, or about ten days long, since the Sun moves through the zodiac at approximately the rate of one degree per day. (This is not exact because not all of our months contain thirty days.)

The decanate of a sign does not change the basic characteristics of that sign, but it does refine and individualize the sign's general characteristics. If you were born, say, in the second decanate of Aquarius, it does not change the fact you are an Aquarian. It does indicate that you have somewhat different and special characteristics from those Aquarian people born in the first decanate or the third decanate.

Finally, each decanate has a specific planetary ruler, sometimes called a subruler because it does not usurp the overall rulership of your sign. The subruler can only enhance and add to the distinct characteristics of your decanate. For example, your entire sign of Aquarius is ruled by Uranus, but the second decanate of Aquarius is subruled by Mercury. The influence of Mercury, the subruler, combines with the overall authority of Uranus to make the second decanate of Aquarius unlike any other in the zodiac.

FIRST DECANATE OF AQUARIUS

January 20 through January 29
Keyword: Knowledge
Constellation: Delphinus, the Dolphin, ancient savior of the ship-
    wrecked. The Dolphin symbolizes spirituality.
Planetary Subruler: Uranus

Uranus, planet of originality, is both your ruler and subruler,
which accentuates your perception and quick mentality. You are
capable and intelligent and deal easily with people. Your wit and
sense of humor are advantages both socially and in your work.
What others may consider obstacles, you think of as challenges.
Finding solutions and a better, quicker way of handling things
is what you emphasize. You are intrigued by new problems and
need change in your activities to keep you from going stale. You
have an affectionate and kindhearted nature, although a lover may
complain of your detachment. This is probably because you try to
apply logic to emotional situations. You are fond of analyzing why
a person behaves in this way or that.

SECOND DECANATE OF AQUARIUS

January 30 through February 8
Keyword: Frankness
Constellation: Piscis Austrinus, the Southern Fish that symbol-
    izes knowledge and fertility of mind. The Fish drinks from the
    Fountain of Wisdom.
Planetary Subruler: Mercury

Mercury, planet of versatility, adds its energy to Aquarius's Uranus, which gives a liveliness and sparkle to your personality. You have a spontaneity and genuine warmth that draw others to you. One of your most outstanding traits is your honesty and frankness in speech. People know they can depend on what you say, for you speak your true mind. Mercury bestows a gift for language, and you may have literary interests. You probably have the ability to sum up a person or situation in a clever and witty phrase. You enjoy knowledge for its own sake and are always interested in learning more. You want love to be a consuming and passionate experience, but you are too self-sufficient to be swept away.

THIRD DECANATE OF AQUARIUS

February 9 through February 18
Keyword: Association
Constellation: Equuleus, the Little Horse, brother of Pegasus. The Little Horse symbolizes loyalty and the harnessing of strength.
Planetary Subruler: Venus

Venus, planet of sociability, combines with Aquarius's Uranus to make you the most people-oriented of the three decanates. You have the ability to form close and enduring ties. Often your success in work comes through other people. You probably have an artistic nature and take pride in making your surroundings as beautiful as you can. You like people who do what they say they will and who show up on time. In your own life, you are careful about details and tend to be critical about the lax ways of others. Travel and new adventure always excite you, for you are a forward-looking person. In love, you are romantic and affectionate, and you tend to have a flirtatious eye.

WHAT IS A CUSP?

A cusp is the point at which a new astrological sign begins.* Thus, the cusp of Aquarius means the point at which Aquarius begins. (The word comes from the Latin word *cuspis*, meaning "point.")

When someone speaks of being "born on the cusp," that person is referring to a birth time at or near the beginning or the end of an astrological sign. For example, if you were born on February 18, you were born on the cusp of Pisces, the sign that begins on February 19. Indeed, depending on what year you were born, your birth time might even be in the first degree of Pisces. People born on the very day a sign begins or ends are often confused about what sign they really are—a confusion made more complicated by the fact that the Sun does not move into or out of a sign at *exactly* the same moment (or even day) each year. There are slight time differences from year to year. Therefore, if you are an Aquarian born on January 20 or February 18, you'll find great clarity consulting a computer chart that tells you exactly where the Sun was at the very moment you were born.

As for what span of time constitutes being born on the cusp, the astrological community holds various opinions. Some astrologers claim cusp means being born only within the first two days or last two days of a sign (though many say this is too narrow a time frame). Others say it can be as much as within the first

*In a birth chart, a cusp is also the point at which an astrological House begins.

ten days or last ten days of a sign (which many say is too wide an interpretation). The consensus is that you were born on the cusp if your birthday is within the first *five* days or last *five* days of a sign.

The question hanging over cusp-born people is "What sign am I really?" They feel they straddle the border of two different countries. To some extent, this is true. If you were born on the cusp, you're under the influence of both signs. However, much like being a traveler leaving one country and crossing into another, you must actually *be* in one country—you can't be in two countries at the same time. One sign is always a stronger influence, and that sign is almost invariably the sign that the Sun was actually in (in other words, your Sun sign). The reason I say "almost" is that in rare cases a chart may be so heavily weighted with planets in a certain sign that the person more keenly feels the influence of that specific sign.

For example, I have a client who was born in the late evening on February 18. On that evening, the Sun was leaving Aquarius and entering Pisces. At the moment of her birth, the Sun was still in Aquarius, so technically speaking she is an Aquarian. However, the Sun was only a couple hours away from being in Pisces, and this person has the Moon, Mercury, and Venus all in Pisces. She has always felt like a Pisces and always behaved as a Pisces.

This, obviously, is an unusual case. Generally, the Sun is the most powerful planetary influence in a chart. Even if you were born with the Sun on the very tip of the first or last degree of Aquarius, Aquarius is your Sun sign—and this is the sign you will most feel like.

Still, the influence of the approaching sign or of the sign just ending is present, and you will probably sense that mixture in yourself.

BORN JANUARY 20 THROUGH JANUARY 24

You are Aquarius with Capricorn tendencies. You have a quick mind and are versatile enough to handle many varied projects. In addition you have a good memory and a methodical approach. Generally, you are most successful in enterprises where you can run things your own way. Your sociable nature attracts people, and you may be known for a witty sense of humor. At times you need complete privacy and periods of reflection. You have a strong streak of independence. You try to deal with love analytically because you dislike falling prey to feelings.

BORN FEBRUARY 14 THROUGH FEBRUARY 18

You are Aquarius with Pisces tendencies. You have an easygoing charm that fits in well with almost any group. Whereas you may have many acquaintances, those who know you really well are few. You have a lighthearted exterior that often hides deeper feelings. In work you are forward-thinking and progressive, but also cautious. You view life with a somewhat jaded eye and won't rush into anything new without investigation. Nothing offends you more than being unfairly dealt with. You tend to have extravagant tastes and enjoy spending money.

YOUR SPECIAL DAY OF BIRTH

JANUARY 20

You're an interesting mix of waywardness and modesty. You carve your own path but are not a showoff. What interests you are ideas that take a project out of the ordinary. In love, you're fond of cuddles, kisses, and passion; you can be flirtatious.

JANUARY 21

You can be an enigma—fiercely determined, often obsessive, and also warmhearted, sentimental, and fun-loving. Primarily you're a traditionalist who wants a secure life. In love, you tend to give your heart too soon; you need to learn romantic balance.

JANUARY 22

Reserved yet talkative, you have a talent for innovative thinking—though you probably won't believe you're brilliant until after you're thirty-five. Emotionally, early on you're a wandering gypsy, and finally, with instant recognition, you'll find your true love.

JANUARY 23

Flair and style are your trademarks; you have a sense of creative magic. You're a potent combination of imagination and sensuality, which is not only physical but in your work and the things you collect. In love, you have true courage, and your life reads like a novel.

JANUARY 24

You're restless, extremely bright, and not destined to be poor (no matter where you start from). Because of childhood experiences, your head and heart are often split, but in time you'll come to deep serenity. In love, you need a best friend who puts you first.

JANUARY 25

People see you as fey and different because your interests are off-beat. But you're an achiever who'll make a mark in a specialized area. You have a gift for relationships: Friendships are long lasting, and your lover is (will be) someone of unusual depth.

JANUARY 26

You're sunny on the outside and deeply feeling on the inside. Being multitalented, it takes a while to find your true calling. Eventually, you'll create a masterpiece. Romantically, you have a tendency to choose lovers who seem strong and turn out not to be.

JANUARY 27

Charismatic and attention-getting, you have real people-power. You radiate strong confidence even though, secretly, you question yourself. You have a caring, nurturing side that comes out when someone needs you. In love, you search for your "other half."

JANUARY 28

You have dazzling charm, and the nicest thing is you don't use this to manipulate. You're true to your commitments and courageous about your principles. In work, you need a burning passion (which you're destined to find). In love, early struggle has made you wise.

JANUARY 29

You're vivacious and intense, a mesmerizing combination that draws people to you. You're not afraid to jump into controversy to find out the truth. In a career, you're a self-starter drawn to unusual areas. Emotionally, you're passionate, with great capacity to love.

JANUARY 30

In day-to-day activities, you prefer the practical and efficient. But your heart yearns for something wild and magical—and you'll find the mate who offers this. You're best at work that shows off your taste and captivating skill with people.

JANUARY 31

You're quick, communicative, and brilliant. What drives you is restlessness (you also tend to be an insomniac), and your search for a grand endeavor will bring you to an unusual place. In love, you're totally devoted, though you give the impression of detachment.

FEBRUARY 1

It takes discipline (which you have lots of) not to get lost in dreams—but you're both a visionary *and* go-getter, which makes you remarkable. You always bring a project to the next level. In affairs of the heart, you're passionate and vulnerable, and need to choose with care.

FEBRUARY 2

Creatively, you draw inspiration from a secret source—your rich inner life. Your work has warmth that touches others. In romantic affairs, you often end up playing the therapist (you understand the human heart well), but you need to be with someone who understands *you*.

FEBRUARY 3

Your natural rapport with people is a great asset in a career—and your high intellect and deep creativity lead you to work that expresses freedom and also makes money. As for love, you hate feeling lonely but have learned not to court unhappiness with the wrong partner.

FEBRUARY 4

Privately you worry, though few know this. Mostly, you're seen as a confident intellectual who communicates effectively and has high ambitions. Emotionally, you're complicated: sensitive, sensual, and restless. You can be a handful to be in love with.

FEBRUARY 5

You have all the qualities of a rebel: feistiness, curiosity, willingness to stick out your neck. By following your instincts, you'll never make a wrong choice. In love, you're devoted in your fashion, but you need lots of passion, stimulation, and adventure.

FEBRUARY 6

Your great strengths are your analytical mind, wit, and perceptiveness about people. In a career, you are brilliant in start-up projects that call for cool poise and hot new ideas. Romantically, you want security *and* intrigue, which doesn't always go together.

FEBRUARY 7

What makes you interesting is you're interested in others. Actually, you learn about yourself this way because you're many people rolled into one. You have amazing talents and a philosophical turn of mind. You're a sensual lover with a flair for the poetic.

FEBRUARY 8

You have an uncanny knack for seizing the emotions of an audience, which makes you a magnetic "showperson." You're destined to be unforgettable. Love tends to be complicated because you're highly individual and dramatic, and need a multilayered partner.

FEBRUARY 9

You're outspoken and a bit of a screwball, which people love. In your work, you're able to capture a part of the past and bring it into a future trend. You can capitalize on this financially. In love, you have a tendency to be a rescuer, though you need someone strong.

FEBRUARY 10

With your effervescent *joie de vivre*, you're a compelling presence. Oddly, though, you're shy, which you cover well. You have a perfectionist drive you should turn into one-of-a-kind work; otherwise you'll waste it. In love, you're ardent, devoted, and deeply romantic.

FEBRUARY 11

You have a commanding presence and an impish heart, a lovely combination that gives you purpose, warmth, and star quality. In your work, communication is your strong point. In love, you exhibit trust and tenderness; just be careful not to mythologize your lovers.

FEBRUARY 12

Though you fret about details, you believe in your ability to make everything come out okay. This conviction gives you freedom to put true authenticity into your work. In love, you have immense courage and more passionate emotionalism than is typical of Aquarius.

FEBRUARY 13

Sensitive and hugely insightful, you're like a spy listening to others and gleaning information. What you learn gives you wisdom about life, and knowledge always leads to self-empowerment. You're a rich tapestry of desire, protectiveness, and a wild, roving heart.

FEBRUARY 14

You're not good at taking orders but are so genial others seem not to notice. You're a sweet maverick with great personal power. Born this day of love, you're a lover through and through. When you connect with the one who sees your heart, you release your passion.

FEBRUARY 15

Under your cool exterior, you're a firebrand who can change the way things are. You have ambition and super intelligence, and you can influence people. You also have luck—what you need appears when you need it. Your emotions are deep, and sexually you can be impulsive.

FEBRUARY 16

With your flair, you create excitement out of ordinary events. Indeed, nothing is ordinary in your life. In a career, you're drawn to unusual people, and in romance you find complicated dramas to get into. Ultimately, you'll be in an intense bond with someone you love.

FEBRUARY 17

You're complex—an individualist who's very social, and an ambitious achiever possessing great warmth. Your work will be memorable. In love, you long for passionate intensity but tend to choose more friendship-type affairs because they're easier.

FEBRUARY 18

People find you very engaged or very distant, nothing in between. You have to be *captivated* by an endeavor or you're completely uninterested. Your skills take you into untried paths. In love, you're sensitive and ultraconsiderate, yet you have a wildly sensual, hedonistic streak.

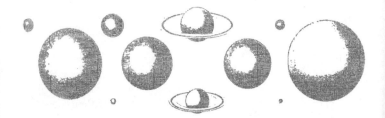

YOU AND CHINESE ASTROLOGY

With Marco Polo's adventurous travels in A.D. 1275, Europeans learned for the first time of the great beauty, wealth, history, and romance of China. Untouched as they were by outside influences, the Chinese developed their astrology along different lines from other ancient cultures, such as the Egyptians, Babylonians, and Greeks in whom Western astrology has its roots. Therefore, the Chinese zodiac differs from the zodiac of the West. To begin with, it is based on a lunar cycle rather than Western astrology's solar cycle. The Chinese zodiac is divided into twelve years, and each year is represented by a different animal—the rat, ox, tiger, rabbit, dragon, snake, horse, goat, monkey, rooster, dog, and pig. The legend of the twelve animals is that when Buddha lay on his deathbed, he asked the animals of the forest to come and bid him farewell. These twelve were the first to arrive. The cat, as the story goes, is not among the animals because it was napping and couldn't be bothered to make the journey. (In some Asian countries, however, such as Vietnam, the cat replaces the rabbit.)

Like Western astrology in which the zodiac signs have different characteristics, each of the twelve Chinese animal years assigns character traits specific to a person born in that year. For example, the Year of the Rat confers honesty and an analytical mind, whereas the Year of the Monkey grants charm and quick ability to take advantage.

Here are descriptions for Aquarius for each Chinese animal year.

Important Note: Our Western year is solar and always begins on January 1. But the Asian year is lunar and always begins on the second new moon after the winter solstice. This means it can begin anywhere from very late in January to middle February. Therefore, Aquarius, you need to know the exact date a specific Asian year began in order to know which animal year you were born in. Under each Chinese year, I have listed some of these dates, but for the years not noted, you will have to do some research.

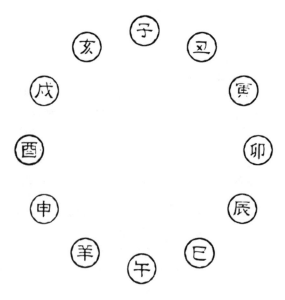

IF YOU ARE AQUARIUS BORN IN THE YEAR OF THE RAT

Years of the Rat

31 Jan 1900 to 18 Feb 1901	15 Feb 1972 to 2 Feb 1973	2044
18 Feb 1912 to 5 Feb 1913	2 Feb 1984 to 19 Feb 1985	2056
5 Feb 1924 to 24 Jan 1925	19 Feb 1996 to 6 Feb 1997	2068
24 Jan 1936 to 10 Feb 1937	7 Feb 2008 to 25 Jan 2009	2080
10 Feb 1948 to 28 Jan 1949	2020	2092
28 Jan 1960 to 14 Feb 1961	2032	

In the West, the rat is considered dirty and repulsive, but the Chinese Rat is full of charm and imagination. The Rat is known for its foresight, creativity, and restless spirit—and this, combined with your offbeat Aquarian nonconformism, produces a daring trailblazer and an intellectual virtuoso. Your drive is to understand the world. You've been affectionately called the "maddest" of all Aquarians, for you're willing to take outrageous risks and rush off on adventures that seem foolhardy to the average person. As an Aquarius Rat, you also have a wild sense of humor and a way of puncturing people's pomposities. You can be a meddler and complainer and a bit of a conniver, but your heart is jolly and you're fun. As a lover, you're generous and sentimental, and if needed you will put the happiness of the one you love ahead of yours. Compatible partners are born in the Years of the Monkey, Pig, Rat, and Snake.

IF YOU ARE AQUARIUS BORN IN THE YEAR OF THE OX

Years of the Ox

19 Feb 1901 to 7 Feb 1902	3 Feb 1973 to 22 Jan 19 1974	2045
6 Feb 1913 to 25 Jan 1914	20 Feb 1985 to 8 Feb 1986	2057
25 Jan 1925 to 12 Feb 1926	7 Feb 1997 to 27 Jan 1998	2069
11 Feb 1937 to 30 Jan 1938	26 Jan 2009 to 13 Feb 2010	2081
29 Jan 1949 to 16 Feb 1950	2021	2093
15 Feb 1961 to 4 Feb 1962	2033	

The Asian Ox has the strength and determination of the Western ox, but none of its presumed dullness. The Asian Ox is eloquent and gifted, known for inspiring confidence, and loved as a leader and role model. Ox persistence added to Aquarian imagination results in the blend of a visionary and strong-minded realist. As an Aquarius Ox, you have an expansive worldview tied to an ability to be practical. In your work, you can create something concrete and enduring that's filled with farsightedness. It's as if you know what will be needed in the future, and this sets you apart. You're original and intellectual, a fast-track progressive, and a deeply caring champion for those you care for. In love, you're a romantic gem—giving and totally devoted for the long haul. You're also an exceptionally sensual lover. Compatible partners are born in the Years of the Rabbit, Rooster, Monkey, Pig, and Snake.

IF YOU ARE AQUARIUS BORN IN THE YEAR OF THE TIGER

Years of the Tiger

8 Feb 1902 to 28 Jan 1903	23 Jan 1974 to 10 Feb 1975	2046
26 Jan 1914 to 13 Feb 1915	9 Feb 1986 to 28 Jan 1987	2058
13 Feb 1926 to 1 Feb 1927	28 Jan 1998 to 15 Feb 1999	2070
31 Jan 1938 to 18 Feb 1939	14 Feb 2010 to 2 Feb 2011	2082
17 Feb 1950 to 5 Feb 1951	2022	2094
5 Feb 1962 to 24 Jan 1963	2034	

In China, the Tiger is venerated for its nobility and authority, and to Buddhists it symbolizes the power of faith. The Tiger has courage and magnetism, and being born in a Tiger year gives you mastery over your environment. Tiger fervor ignites your Aquarius intellectual brilliance, and you have the daring to rush toward major challenges. To others, you can seem imperious and arrogant, but this is because you zoom into situations assuming you know everything. At heart you're a romantic visionary—you want to sweep out stodgy thinking and implement idealistic ventures. You're a hardworking, often eccentric entrepreneur. Love brings out your exuberant generosity, though you keep looking for the impossible dream. As long as a relationship contains passion and excitement, you tend not to stray. Compatible partners are born in the Years of the Rabbit, Dog, Dragon, Monkey, Tiger, and Pig.

IF YOU ARE AQUARIUS BORN IN THE YEAR OF THE RABBIT

Years of the Rabbit

29 Jan 1903 to 15 Feb 1904	11 Feb 1975 to 30 Jan 1976	2047
14 Feb 1915 to 2 Feb 1916	29 Jan 1987 to 16 Feb 1988	2059
2 Feb 1927 to 22 Jan 1928	16 Feb 1999 to 4 Feb 2000	2071
19 Feb 1939 to 7 Feb 1940	3 Feb 2011 to 22 Jan 2012	2083
6 Feb 1951 to 26 Jan 1952	2023	2095
25 Jan 1963 to 12 Feb 1964	2035	

The Asian Rabbit (or, in countries such as Vietnam, the Cat) is refined, ambitious, wise, and delightfully creative. The Rabbit has elegant taste and resourceful imagination, and its theatrical quality magnifies Aquarian ability to stand out as an individual. You shine in large groups and have a talent for work in which you put different personalities together. You're less interested in money than in unusual and untried ideas, though luckily you often land in lucrative situations. As an Aquarius Rabbit, it's true you can be a purist and elitist—and some think you're superficial, no doubt because you detach from their dramas. Even in your own emotional life, you're not fond of *Sturm und Drang*. You'd like love to be affectionate and fun, with lots of mental and sexual companionship. Compatible partners are born in the Years of the Goat, Dog, Dragon, Snake, Horse, and Monkey.

IF YOU ARE AQUARIUS BORN IN THE YEAR OF THE DRAGON

Years of the Dragon

19 Feb 1904 to 3 Feb 1905	31 Jan 1976 to 17 Feb 1977	2048
3 Feb 1916 to 22 Jan 1917	17 Feb 1988 to 5 Feb 1989	2060
23 Jan 1928 to 9 Feb 1929	5 Feb 2000 to 23 Jan 2001	2072
8 Feb 1940 to 26 Jan 1941	23 Jan 2012 to 9 Feb 2013	2084
27 Jan 1952 to 13 Feb 1953	2024	2096
13 Feb 1964 to 1 Feb 1965	2036	

The Asian Dragon is a mythic creature of power, sovereignty, and spirituality. The Dragon personifies life force (what the Chinese call *Ch'i*) and symbolizes the realization of ideals. Dragon willpower combines with Aquarian genius to create an idealistic rebel with a special destiny to rule a kingdom (usually a one-of-a-kind creative enterprise). The Year of the Dragon always blows in change, and as an Aquarius Dragon you shift everything around (people's opinions, old ways of doing things) and stand out as a powerhouse innovator. This is true in your work, relationships, and lifestyle. In love, you're a giver and helper; you're very caring. You look for a confidante and companion through life but, in fact, tend to be a rescuer. Take care not to settle for someone weaker than you. Compatible partners are born in the Years of the Rabbit, Goat, Monkey, Snake, and Tiger.

IF YOU ARE AQUARIUS BORN IN THE YEAR OF THE SNAKE

Years of the Snake

4 Feb 1905 to 24 Jan 1906	18 Feb 1977 6 Feb 1978	2049
23 Jan 1917 10 Feb 1918	6 Feb 1989 to 26 Jan 1990	2061
10 Feb 1929 29 Jan 1930	24 Jan 2001 to 11 Feb 2002	2073
27 Jan 1941 14 Feb 1942	10 Feb 2013 to 30 Jan 2014	2085
14 Feb 1953 to 2 Feb 1954	2025	2097
2 Feb 1965 to 20 Jan 1966	2037	

The Asian Snake is artistic, fluent, highly intelligent—linked to the Goddess of Beauty and the Sea. The Snake is an elegant charmer and very smart about survival (Chinese believe that if a Snake person is part of the household, the family will never starve). Snake's restless independence merges seamlessly with your inventive Aquarian imagination, and you are blessed with an extra-clever brain and willingness to explore. As an Aquarius Snake, you're said to be both light and dark—in the sense that you have star-quality radiance when dealing with people and are also a complicated person of desire, secrets, and unexpressed competitiveness. You work "undercover" toward your goals and always achieve them. In love, you long for completion (which you will find), and as you mature you learn to be less controlling. Compatible partners are born in the Years of the Rabbit, Rooster, Dragon, Horse, Ox, and Rat.

IF YOU ARE AQUARIUS BORN IN THE YEAR OF THE HORSE

Years of the Horse

25 Jan 1906 12 Feb 1907	7 Feb 1978 to 27 Jan 1979	2050
11 Feb 1918 to 31 Jan 1919	27 Jan 1990 to 14 Feb 1991	2062
30 Jan 1930 to 16 Feb 1931	12 Feb 2002 to 31 Jan 2003	2074
15 Feb 1942 to 4 Feb 1943	31 Jan 2014 18 Feb 2015	2086
3 Feb 1954 to 23 Jan 1955	2026	2098
21 Jan 1966 8 Feb 1967	2038	

In Asia, the Horse is so powerful that pregnancies are planned around a Horse year. The Horse is extroverted, charismatic, has boldness and bravura, and represents the principle of speed. The Horse's joyful life force combines with your Aquarian prophetic vision—synergizing into a take-charge leader with a wildly adventurous heart. You don't look to lead people, but they follow you anyway because you do things on a grand scale. As an Aquarius Horse, you explore the far reaches of the imagination and still manage to build secure foundations. Still, your Achilles' heel can be money; dissipation and disorganization run through your character. In love, you're quick tinder and adore passionate encounters. If only long-term commitment were as exciting as combustible sex, your love life would be perfect. Compatible partners are born in the Years of the Rabbit, Rooster, Goat, Horse, and Snake.

IF YOU ARE AQUARIUS BORN IN THE YEAR OF THE GOAT

Years of the Goat

13 Feb 1907 to 1 Feb 1908	28 Jan 1979 to 15 Feb 1980	2051
1 Feb 1919 to 19 Feb 1920	15 Feb 1991 to 3 Feb 1992	2063
17 Feb 1931 to 5 Feb 1932	1 Feb 2003 to 21 Jan 2004	2075
5 Feb 1943 to 24 Jan 1944	19 Feb 2015 to 7 Feb 2016	2087
24 Jan 1955 to 11 Feb 1956	2027	2099
9 Feb 1967 to 29 Jan 1968	2039	

The Goat is captivating and lovable, one of the most engaging signs of the Chinese zodiac. Known for its quick mind and artistic flair, the Goat has a wayward, whimsical approach to life and, luckily, attracts breaks and blessings from all kinds of sources. Goat adaptability blends superbly with Aquarian creativity, making you more fluid than many Aquarians. Aquarius Goat has been called "lighter than air," which describes not only how you think but the ease with which you glide into a crowd and imperceptibly change their direction. A streak of dissatisfaction runs through you, and certainly you're undisciplined, but you have spunk, energy, and a touch of the mad poet. In love especially, you're a great romantic and an exciting lover, though it takes patience and understanding to get you to settle down. Compatible partners are born in the Years of the Rabbit, Dragon, Horse, Monkey, and Pig.

IF YOU ARE AQUARIUS BORN IN THE YEAR OF THE MONKEY

Years of the Monkey

2 Feb 1908 to 21 Jan 1909	16 Feb 1980 to 4 Feb 1981	2052
20 Feb 1920 to 7 Feb 1921	4 Feb 1992 to 22 Jan 1993	2064
6 Feb 1932 to 25 Jan 1933	22 Jan 2004 to 8 Feb 2005	2076
25 Jan 1944 to 12 Feb 1945	8 Feb 2016 to 27 Jan 2017	2088
12 Feb 1956 to 30 Jan 1957	2028	2100
29 Jan 1968 16 Feb 1969	2040	

In Asian lore, the entertaining Monkey was the beloved companion to the God of Sailors on long sea voyages. Vivacious, witty, clever, highly sociable, and a bit of con man, the Monkey has effervescent rapport with people. Monkey liveliness and curiosity magnify your quicksilver Aquarian intellect, making you a brilliant communicator. Your brain works at warp speed. Still, you can be an erratic genius because you like to come and go and not be inextricably caught in any one thing. You're a restless bird of youth. If it weren't for your Aquarian honesty, you'd be quite a manipulator, for you have an opportunistic nature and a way of divulging only what someone needs to know. You have a generous heart, though, and in love particularly, are caring and honorable in spite of your flirtatiousness. Compatible partners are born in the Years of the Rabbit, Dragon, Ox, Pig, Rat, and Tiger.

IF YOU ARE AQUARIUS BORN IN THE YEAR OF THE ROOSTER

Years of the Rooster

22 Jan 1909 to 9 Feb 1910	5 Feb 1981 to 24 Jan 1982	2053
8 Feb 1921 to 27 Jan 1922	23 Jan 1993 to 9 Feb 1994	2065
26 Jan 1933 to 13 Feb 1934	9 Feb 2005 to 28 Jan 2006	2077
13 Feb 1945 to 1 Feb 1946	28 Jan 2017 15 Feb 2018	2089
31 Jan 1957 to 17 Feb 1958	2029	
17 Feb 1969 to 5 Feb 1970	2041	

The Rooster symbolizes courage and, in Eastern mythology, was the brave being who rescued the Goddess of the Sun. The Rooster is high-minded, sincere, outspoken, and not afraid to confront—qualities that give double force to your Aquarian firebrand energy. The Year of the Rooster always ushers in reform and improvement, and as an Aquarius Rooster your life bent is to change what doesn't work and expand people's thinking. You enjoy your reputation as an oddball. There's something of the detective and psychoanalyst in you—you like to get to a hidden truth and then flash on an idea others haven't thought of. Your ability to probe and "peck away" is valuable in your work as researcher and creator (you're both). In love, you're deeply romantic yet tend to put up defenses. But when you give your heart away, your promise is forever. Compatible partners are born in the Years of the Horse, Ox, and Snake.

IF YOU ARE AQUARIUS BORN IN THE YEAR OF THE DOG

(戌)

Years of the Dog

10 Feb 1910 to 29 Jan 1911	25 Jan 1982 to 12 Feb 1983	2054
28 Jan 1922 to 15 Feb 1923	10 Feb 1994 to 30 Jan 1995	2066
14 Feb 1934 to 3 Feb 1935	29 Jan 2006 to 17 Feb 2007	2078
2 Feb 1946 to 21 Jan 1947	16 Feb 2018 to 4 Feb 2019	2090
18 Feb 1958 to 7 Feb 1959	2030	
6 Feb 1970 to 26 Jan 1971	2042	

Exactly as its real-life counterpart, the Asian Dog is faithful, devoted, and loyal to the end. Imbued with heroism and a sense of duty, the Dog takes care of others. Exhibiting the finer traits of human nature, the Dog inspires confidence. Dog's "guard-dog" energy sparks your Aquarian instinct for fixing the world, making you extra vigilant about doing the right thing and rooting out people's wrong thinking. Certainly your aspirations are noble, but you're also a worrier and nagger when you see others messing up. Yes, your bark is as bad as your bite, for when you don't get your way, you can be quite assertive. Still, as an Aquarius Dog, you are a powerful force for good and in your work exhibit caring, vision, and creative panache. In love, passion and feelings steam up in you, but you can be jealous and overprotective. Compatible partners are born in the Years of the Cat, Dog, Pig, and Tiger.

IF YOU ARE AQUARIUS BORN IN THE YEAR OF THE PIG

Years of the Pig

30 Jan 1911 to 17 Feb 1912	13 Feb 1983 to 1 Feb 1984	2055
16 Feb 1923 to 4 Feb 1924	31 Jan 1995 to 18 Feb 1996	2067
4 Feb 1935 to 23 Jan 1936	18 Feb 2007 to 6 Feb 2008	2079
22 Jan 1947 to 9 Feb 1948	5 Feb 2019 to 24 Jan 2020	2091
8 Feb 1959 to 27 Jan 1960	2031	
27 Jan 1971 to 15 Feb 1972	2043	

In the West, the lowly pig is scorned, but the Asian Pig is gallant and chivalrous, honest and knowledgeable. The Pig represents enlightenment—the Pig's clear thinking enhances your Aquarian mental skills, resulting in a bona fide "whiz kid." You're always young at heart and have kid energy, but you're also a wise seer. These qualities of quickness and seeing keep you from getting sucked into people's crazy dramas. As an Aquarius Pig, you have stubborn stick-to-it-iveness that's a great advantage in a career, especially any work in which you're breaking new ground. You'll always make a splash in the public. As for love, here your heart can be too trusting and sometimes suffer early heartbreak. But you'll end up with someone who loves the true pilgrim soul in you. Compatible partners are born in the Years of the Rabbit, Dog, Pig, Ox, and Tiger.

YOU AND NUMEROLOGY

Numerology is the language of numbers. It is the belief that there is a correlation between numbers and living things, ideas, and concepts. Certainly, numbers surround and infuse our lives (e.g., twenty-four hours in a day, twelve months of the year, etc.). And from ancient times, mystics have taught that numbers carry a *vibration*, a deeper meaning that defines how each of us fits into the universe. According to numerology, you are born with a personal number that contains information about who you are and what you need to be happy. This number expresses what numerology calls your life path.

All numbers reduce to one of nine digits, numbers 1 through 9. Your personal number is based on your date of birth. To calculate your number, write your birth date in numerals. As an example, the birth date of January 30, 1987, is written 1-30-1987. Now begin the addition: 1 + 30 + 1 + 9 + 8 + 7 = 56; 56 reduces to 5 + 6 = 11; 11 reduces to 1 + 1 = 2. The personal number for someone born on January 30, 1987, is *Two*.

IF YOU ARE AN AQUARIUS ONE

Keywords: Confidence and Creativity

One is the number of leadership and new beginnings. You rush into whatever engages your heart—whether a new plan, a love affair, or an adventurous trip. You're courageous, inventive, and an ambitious optimist. You're attracted to unusual creative pursuits because you like to be one of a kind. You can't bear to be under the thumb of other people's whims and agendas. The best careers for you are those in which you're in charge and able to work independently. As for love, you want ecstasy and passion and can be a roses-and-champagne romantic. The most exciting part of an affair is the beginning, but you also have staying power.

IF YOU ARE AN AQUARIUS TWO

Keywords: Cooperation and Balance

Two is the number of cooperation and creating a secure entity. Being a Two gives you extra Aquarian magnetism—you attract what you need. Your magic is not only your people skills, but your ability to breathe life into empty forms (e.g., a concept, an ambitious business idea, a new relationship) and produce something of worth. In your work, you're a perfectionist—and because you have both a creative side *and* a practical side, you're drawn to careers that combine a business sense with an artistic challenge. In love, your deepest desire is for a loving partnership with someone you can trust and share confidences with.

IF YOU ARE AN AQUARIUS THREE

Keywords: Expression and Sensitivity

Three symbolizes self-expression. Being a Three magnifies your gift for words and your talent for seeing the possibilities that exist. You link people together so that they benefit from each other. You stimulate others to think. Because you're a connector, you're much loved as a leader, spokesperson, and friend. In a career, Aquarian creativity and innovation are your specialties. You're a quick study, mentally active, and curious about the new. In love, you need someone who excites you intellectually and sensually, and understands your complex personality. Casual acquaintances may not see your depth, but in love you must have a soulmate who does.

IF YOU ARE AN AQUARIUS FOUR

Keywords: Stability and Process

Four is the number of dedication and loyalty. It represents *foundation*, exactly as a four-sided square does. You like to build, and the direction you go in is up. As a Four, your Aquarian fixity is underlined—you want to create something of value, and you have persistence. Therefore, you're able to accomplish great works. You look for self-expression in your craft and are at your best when you can go at your own pace without others interfering. Sexually, you're an imaginative and generous lover, and you need a giving and understanding partner with whom you can express your rich sensuality.

IF YOU ARE AN AQUARIUS FIVE

Keywords: Freedom and Discipline

Five is the number of change and freedom. You're a gregarious nonconformist. With your chameleon intellect (it can go in any direction) and captivating ability to deal with people, you're a marvelous *persuader*. You charm and influence others and have power with the public. In friendships, you're quick to jump in to give advice and whatever the other needs. Your deepest desire is to push past boundaries and express your free spirit. This is true sexually, as well, and you are a most inventive lover. But when you give your heart away for keeps, it's to someone with whom you passionately mesh—body and mind.

IF YOU ARE AN AQUARIUS SIX

Keywords: Vision and Acceptance

Six is the number of teaching, healing, and utilizing your talents. You're geared toward changing the world, or at least fixing other people's lives. Being an advice giver and even a therapist to your friends comes naturally. In addition, you're exacting—especially with yourself. You hold to high standards and bring an artisan's excellence to everything you do. Being a Six magnifies your humanitarian instincts, so you also bring uplifting energy to others. In love, you're fervent about being a helpmate and confidante. You're a true partner as well as a passionate sensualist who gives your all to someone you trust.

IF YOU ARE AN AQUARIUS SEVEN

Keywords: Trust and Openness

Seven is the number of the mystic and the intensely focused specialist. You observe and, by analyzing, gain wisdom. You have an instinct for problem solving, and in a flash understand how things work (in business, between people, etc.). You enjoy communicating your ideas and putting them to use. You're an intellectual and connoisseur of everything creative. You pursue *self*-determination (not being controlled by outside forces). At your core, you're extremely loyal and intensely loving, though very selective about relationships. In love, your deepest need is for a partner who can help you on your life's journey.

IF YOU ARE AN AQUARIUS EIGHT

Keywords: Abundance and Power

Eight is the number of mastery and authority. You are intelligent, alert, quick in action, born to take control in your own hands and guide traffic into the direction you want. You work well with groups because you see what's needed and can delegate (a major success tool). You're also a good judge of character. Others sense you're the one who knows best, and they're right. As an Aquarius Eight, you're likely to reach out to diversified groups, travel, and add to your education. Giving your promise in love is a serious act. You're a protective and caring lover, and in turn you need to know your lover is your loyal ally.

IF YOU ARE AN AQUARIUS NINE

Keywords: Integrity and Wisdom

Nine is the path of the "old soul," the number of completion and full bloom. Because it's the last number, it sums up the highs and lows of human experience, and you live a life of dramatic events. People see you as colorful and heroic because you have an adventurous outlook but are also spiritual and altruistic. You're intellectual, interested in all kinds of exploration, do highly original work, and are an inspiration to others. In love, you're truthful and sincere—and also a romantic, sensual creature. As an Aquarius Nine, you generously give of yourself, often to the point of sacrificing.

LAST WORD: YOUR AQUARIUS UNFINISHED BUSINESS

Psychologists often use the phrase *unfinished business* to describe unresolved issues—for example, patterns from childhood that cause unhappiness, anger that keeps one stuck, scenarios of family dysfunction that repeat through second and third generations (such as alcoholism or abusive behavior).

Astrology teaches that the past is indeed very much with us in the present. And that using astrological insights can help us move out of emotional darkness into greater clarity. Even within this book (which is not a tome of hundreds of pages) you have read of many of the superlatives and challenges of being Aquarius. You have breathtaking gifts and at the same time certain tendencies that can undermine utilizing these abilities.

In nature, a fascinating fact is that in jungles and forests a poisonous plant will grow in a certain spot and always, just a few feet away, is a plant that is the antidote to that specific poison. Likewise, in astrology, the antidote is right there ready to be used when the negatives threaten to overwhelm your life

Aquarius's unfinished business had to do with anger. You're barely in touch with your anger, and yet you feel it without recognizing it. You see yourself as someone terribly nice and understanding, but for all your goodness misunderstood and not seen for who you are. People become irritated with you; they don't want to hear your "truth." They ignore you.

A basic problem is Aquarius's identification with its ideas. Like all Air signs (Gemini, Libra, and Aquarius), your ego is invested in your ideas. You will never see one as fallible. Instead, you try to make reality fit what you think reality *should* be, and when this fails you, you grow morose, further detached, and bitter. It's the fault of the "system"; it's the fault of other people.

Aquarius loves the idea of the betterment of humanity but doesn't love people. Too often, another person is a "something" you're curious about. You don't have a heart connection to the person—your connection is in the head. Because of a cutoff between thinking and feeling, you fail to read the emotions of another. For example, you may lack insight into struggle or pain a lover or family member may be experiencing, and it comes as a shock when this person turns on you and accuses you of not caring. The elements of detachment and separation define your relationships.

A corollary of Aquarius's "blindspot" is difficulty taking responsibility. In your work, in being helpful and altruistic, you are hugely responsible. But in seeing a cause and effect between what you do (or don't do)—especially vis-à-vis relationships—you don't take responsibility. You don't see when your choices create a problem. You retreat into denial.

Denial is exactly how you cope with your anger. You are a cool Aquarian, and to be transformed into someone who rants or screams is unthinkable. You repress anger, and it may turn into physical symptoms or exhibit itself as depression.

Yet the antidotes are there to be found in their entirety in being Aquarius, for you are the sign of effecting changes—the sign of idealistic values and making a difference. When you come to truly know yourself, mentally and emotionally, you are able to expand outward, away from the pettiness that consumes so many. When you can face yourself courageously, you can face any challenge from the outside. With your brilliance and compassion, you're a powerful communicator and activist—not necessarily a political activist, but a force for good in other people's lives. You have a humanitarian heart, one that can love deeply. Aquarius is the sign of needing freedom, and to be really free you must break away from your control patterns and the boundaries you yourself put on you by denying your true feelings. Aquarius, you are the Awakener, and when you awaken to yourself, you live in limitless possibility.

FAMOUS PEOPLE WITH THE SUN IN AQUARIUS

Jennifer Aniston
Susan B. Anthony
Corazon Aquino
Tallulah Bankhead
Mikhail Baryshnikov
John Belushi
Christie Brinkley
Tom Brokaw
George Burns
Robert Burns
Aaron Burr
Lord Byron
Eddie Cantor
Lewis Carroll
Carol Channing
Stockard Channing
Paddy Chayefsky
Natalie Cole
Charles Darwin
Angela Davis
Geena Davis
James Dean
Neil Diamond
Charles Dickens
Matt Dillon
Christian Dior
Placido Domingo
Dr. Dre
Thomas Alva Edison
Sergei Eisenstein
Mia Farrow
Farrah Fawcett
Federico Fellini
W. C. Fields
Clark Gable
Zsa Zsa Gabor
Philip Glass
Christopher Guest
Germaine Greer
Zane Grey

D. W. Griffith
John Grisham
Paris Hilton
Langston Hughes
Holly Hunter
Virginia Johnson-Masters
Michael Jordan
James Joyce
Jerome Kern
Alicia Keys
Nastassja Kinski
Eartha Kitt
Ted Koppel
Mario Lanza
Heath Ledger
Jack Lemmon
Sinclair Lewis
Joseph Lieberman
Abraham Lincoln
Charles Lindbergh
Ernst Lubitsch
Ida Lupino
David Lynch
Douglas MacArthur
John McEnroe
Norman Mailer
Edouard Manet
Christopher Marlowe
W. Somerset Maugham
Felix Mendelssohn
Carmen Miranda
James Michener
Jeanne Moreau
Toni Morrison
Robert Motherwell
Wolfgang Amadeus Mozart
Paul Newman
Jack Nicklaus
Nick Nolte
Kim Novak

Yoko Ono
Thomas Paine
Anna Pavlova
S. J. Perelman
James Pike
Jackson Pollock
Leontyne Price
Ronald Reagan
Vanessa Redgrave
Burt Reynolds
Jackie Robinson
Chris Rock
Norman Rockwell
Franklin Delano Roosevelt
Arthur Rubinstein
Babe Ruth
Telly Savalas
Franz Schubert
Andres Segovia
Tom Selleck
Jane Seymour
Cybill Shepherd
Susan Sontag
Gertrude Stein
Stendhal
George Stephanopoulos
Adlai Stevenson
Justin Timberlake
John Travolta
François Truffaut
Lana Turner
Barbara Tuchman
Jules Verne
Robert Wagner
Edith Wharton
John Williams
Oprah Winfrey
Elijah Wood

PART TWO

ALL ABOUT YOUR SIGN OF AQUARIUS

AQUARIUS'S ASTROLOGICAL AFFINITIES, LINKS, AND LORE

SYMBOL: The Water Bearer

Dispensing a gift that flows freely and equally to all. The Water Bearer represents creation and the giving of life. This association goes back to Sumerian times and the Water Bearer's link to Enki, the God of Creation. Enki was depicted with two streams of water emanating from his shoulders, one symbolizing the Tigris River, the other the Euphrates River.

Often Aquarius is mistakenly thought to be a Water sign. It is an Air sign. The water that the Water Bearer pours out symbolizes truth—which you freely give out to the world.

RULING PLANET: Uranus ⛢

The ancient Greek sky god, first ruler of the universe. This was the first modern planet to be discovered (in 1781) after the invention of the telescope. Uranus is the only planet in our solar system to rotate on its side. Thus, while one hemisphere is continually bathed in sunlight, the other hemisphere is in darkness, and these periods of light and dark each last for twenty-one years at a time. The unusual characteristics of this planet correspond to its astrological reputation for eccentricity.

In astrology, Uranus is the planet of change, disruption, revolutions, the unconventional and unexpected. It is associated with genius and individuality—and rules invention, aerodynamics, and modern science.

DOMINANT KEYWORD

I KNOW

GLYPH (WRITTEN SYMBOL) ≈

The pictograph represents the water that flows from the vessel of the Water Bearer. The glyph shows moving water—a life force akin to electricity. The glyph is also a picture of the human ankle in motion, the part of the anatomy that Aquarius rules. In symbolic terms, the ridged unbroken lines represent electric energy, universal thought, and the wisdom of the future.

PART OF THE BODY RULED BY AQUARIUS:
The Circulatory System, Shins, and Ankles

Aquarians are prone toward ankle sprains and breaks. Also to varicose veins and hardening of the arteries.

LUCKY DAY: Wednesday

Wednesday comes from the Old Norse for Woden's Day (Woden was the god associated with Mercury). Mercury is the planet of the mind. Although Aquarius's ruling planet is Uranus, Uranus was not discovered until 1781, long after the days of the week had been named. Being the sign of mental brilliance, Aquarius was associated by the ancients with Mercury's day of Wednesday.

LUCKY NUMBERS: 1 and 7

Numerologically, 1 is the number of innovation, independence, and courage—and 7 is linked to knowledge, analysis, intellectual curiosity, and deeper understanding. These qualities align with the nature of Aquarius.

TAROT CARD: The Star

The card in the Tarot linked to Aquarius is the Star. Ancient names for this card are Daughters of the Firmament and Dweller Between the Waters. In the Tarot, the card signifies hope and inspiration, and clarity of vision. This is a lucky card to receive in a Tarot reading, for it tells of unexpected help arriving and hopes and wishes coming true. The message is to go forward with courage and confidence toward your goal and have faith in your lucky star.

The card itself pictures a young maiden kneeling by a pond of water with one knee on the ground and one foot in the water. In each hand she holds a pitcher from which she pours water, one onto the land and one into the pool of water. Above her are eight stars. In the card, the ground represents the material world, the pool of water signifies emotion, and the water pouring from the pitchers is life. The stars above symbolize enlightenment and cosmic protection.

For Aquarius, the Star tells you to follow your bliss and that when you take the path of your heart and remain truthful to yourself, the universe will support you.

MAGICAL BIRTHSTONE: Amethyst

A quartz gemstone prized for its sublime lavender-violet-purple color and its use as a talisman, the word *amethyst* comes from the ancient Greek meaning "not intoxicated." This was the gem of sobriety and clear thinking. Its purple color is said to be high-vibrational and thus conducive to peace of mind and balance. The Egyptians placed amethysts over the hearts of the dead to ensure a serene journey to the next life. For Aquarians, the amethyst brings faithfulness in love and bestows the gift of prescience.

SPECIAL COLOR: Electric Blue

The clear color of the sky. Blue symbolizes truth, the intellect, and spaciousness.

CONSTELLATION OF AQUARIUS

Aquarius is the Latin word for Water Bearer and is one of the oldest constellations to be recognized and named. The Sumerians pictured this constellation as their god Enki, who later became the Babylonian god Ea. Ea, known as the "Great One," was depicted holding an overflowing vessel. Both Ea and the earlier Enki represent creation and replenishment. They were embodiments of the Tigris and Euphrates, the location where civilization first began. In Babylonian astronomy, Ea also ruled the "Way of Ea," which was the path along the zodiac that the Sun follows for 45 days after the Winter Solstice. (Since the sign of Capricorn begins on the winter solstice, the mythology of Ea is also linked to Capricorn.)

CITIES

Stockholm, Moscow, Buenos Aires, Salzburg

COUNTRIES

Russia, Sweden, Ethiopia

FLOWER

Orchid

TREES

Fruit trees

HERBS AND SPICES

Those that have sharp flavor

METAL: Uranium

A silvery-white radioactive metal found naturally in the earth and used since early Roman times in glassmaking and pottery. It was only in 1789, however, when science actually "discovered" and then produced uranium in large quantities, that it was named (after the planet Uranus discovered eight years earlier). When combined with other elements, uranium can produce radium (used in treatments for diseases, such as cancer)—and during World War II was combined with plutonium to create atomic energy.

On an esoteric level, the qualities of uranium—such as the ability to radiate (radioactivity) and to bring about nuclear fission—align with the Aquarian gift for futuristic thinking and the capability of understanding things in a flash.

ANIMALS RULED BY AQUARIUS

Large birds

DANGER

Aquarians are innovative, unconventional, and sometimes eccentric, and are therefore often targets for attack by narrow-minded people. Aquarians also have a tendency to get into unusual situations and take up with oddball people.

PERSONAL PROVERBS

Each of us lives a life that has never been, or ever will be, exactly like that of any other human being.

Seek to do good, and you will find that happiness runs after you.

KEYWORDS FOR AQUARIUS

Altruistic
Idealistic
Humanitarian
Hopeful and optimistic
Friendly
Kind and courteous
Loyal
Truthful
Inquisitive
Hungry for knowledge
Abstract thinker

Visionary
Individualistic
Original
Inventive
Broadminded
Imaginative
Explorative and experimental
Freedom-seeking
Independent
Detached
Reformer
Avant-garde
Radical
Unpredictable
Offbeat
Eccentric
Futuristic
Nonmaterialistic

HOW ASTROLOGY SLICES AND DICES YOUR SIGN OF AQUARIUS

DUALITY: Masculine

The twelve astrological signs are divided into two groups, *masculine* and *feminine*. Six are masculine and six are feminine; this is known as the sign's *duality*. A masculine sign is direct and energetic. A feminine sign is receptive and magnetic. These attributes were given to the signs about 2,500 years ago. Today modern astrologers avoid the sexism implicit in these distinctions. A masculine sign does not mean "positive and forceful" any more than a feminine sign means "negative and weak." In modern terminology, the masculine signs, such as your sign of Aquarius, are defined as outer-directed and strong through action. The feminine signs are self-contained and strong through inner reserves.

TRIPLICITY (ELEMENT): Air

The twelve signs are also divided into groups of three signs each. These three-sign groups are called a *triplicity*, and each of these denotes an *element*. The elements are *Fire*, *Earth*, *Air*, and *Water*. In astrology, an element symbolizes a fundamental characterization of the sign.

The three *Fire* signs are Aries, Leo, and Sagittarius. Fire signs are active and enthusiastic.

The three *Earth* signs are Taurus, Virgo, and Capricorn. Earth signs are practical and stable.

The three *Air* signs are Gemini, Libra, and Aquarius. Air signs are intellectual and communicative.

The three *Water* signs are Cancer, Scorpio, and Pisces. Water signs are emotional and intuitive.

QUADRUPLICITY (QUALITY): Fixed

The twelve signs are also divided into groups of four signs each. These four-sign groups are called a *quadruplicity*, and each of these denotes a *quality*. The qualities are *Cardinal*, *Fixed*, and *Mutable*. In astrology, the quality signifies the sign's interaction with the outside world.

Four signs are *Cardinal** signs. They are Aries, Cancer, Libra, and Capricorn. Cardinal signs are enterprising and outgoing. They are the initiators and leaders.

Four signs are *Fixed*. They are Taurus, Leo, Scorpio, and Aquarius. Fixed signs are stubborn, loyal, willful, and they hold on. They are perfectors and finishers, resistant to pressures from the outside (opinions, rules, etc.).

*When the Sun crosses the four cardinal points in the zodiac, we mark the beginning of each of our four seasons. Aries begins spring; Cancer begins summer; Libra begins fall; Capricorn begins winter.

Four signs are *Mutable*. They are Gemini, Virgo, Sagittarius, and Pisces. Mutable signs are flexible, versatile, and adaptable. They are able to adjust to differing circumstances.

Your sign of Aquarius is a Masculine, Air, Fixed sign—and no other sign in the zodiac is this exact combination. Your sign is a one-of-a-kind combination, and therefore you express the characteristics of your duality, element, and quality differently from any other sign.

For example, your sign is a *Masculine* sign, meaning you are active, outgoing, venturesome. You're an *Air* sign, meaning you're intelligent, highly expressive, and fascinated with ideas and knowledge. And you're a *Fixed* sign, meaning you're dedicated, committed, and resolute, and you hold on tenaciously, especially to what you believe in.

Now the sign of Gemini is also Masculine and Air, but unlike Aquarius (which is Fixed), Gemini is Mutable. Like you, Gemini is energetic, on the go, gregarious, and communicative, and especially focused on self-expression. But Gemini will vacillate, hesitate, go off into side-paths, and shrink from commitment. Gemini is flighty, wayward, easily distracted. It resists being pinned down by schedules or promises and doesn't have your adherence to an aim. You, being Fixed, are much more focused. Your fixity is primarily of the mind: You hold to opinions and beliefs. You're a stickler for facts and for the truth. When you set yourself on a course, you don't waver. You're disciplined, though always to a discipline of your own devising, not others'. You're also fixed in your loyalty to friendships, relationships, and causes.

Libra, too, is also Masculine and Air, but unlike Aquarius (which is Fixed), Libra is Cardinal. Like you, Libra is outgoing and expansive, interacts well with people, has high intelligence, and enjoys the exchange of ideas. Especially, Libra has social flair and charm, and uses its articulateness to cultivate relationships. However, being Cardinal, Libra is stirred by the start of something new and filled with grand plans about the endeavor's success. Cardinal energy loves to initiate but doesn't have your Aquarian staying power. Libra is impulsive and enthusiastic, gung ho to begin; its leadership abilities are most pronounced when launching a project. Lacking your fixity though, Libra can grow bored and disenchanted, fizzle out. You, on the other hand, are not easily swayed off course. You have focus and zealotry. Primarily, you fix on a concept you hold dear and important. You can't be talked out of things the way Libra can. Libra is famous for being indecisive and changing its mind. Not you.

POLARITY: Leo

The twelve signs are also divided into groups of two signs each. These two-sign groups are called a *polarity* (meaning "opposite"). Each sign in the zodiac has a polarity, which is its opposite sign in the other half of the zodiac. The two signs express opposite characteristics.

Aquarius and Leo are a polarity. Aquarius is the sign of hopes and dreams, friends and wishes, and you are most engaged in expansive ideas. Aquarians are idealistic humanitarians concerned with the larger issues of the world but have a harder time with intimacy on a personal level. Leo is the sign of pleasure, love affairs, and creative expression. Leos are highly emotional and look for ways to dramatize themselves and to link intimately with others.

Aquarius exhibits an airy kind of detachment, a head in the clouds quality. Aquarius is the sign of impersonal friendliness.

Comradeship and brotherhood are more your thing than intense emotional bonding. Your special gift is for banding a group together for a mutual purpose. You're highly effective in clubs and organizations, for you motivate people to unite together in support of their aims.

You're a champion for causes. Doing good and effecting change motivate you—this is what you're born to accomplish. You want to make the world a better place and are drawn to social and spiritual issues. Idealism and activism are part of your Aquarian character. In essence, Aquarius gives with open arms to larger principles and wider groups. One-on-one dealings are more challenging.

You are, however, gifted at friendship—generally, friendship (not necessarily love) is a commitment for life. Even if circumstances keep you and a friend apart, you can renew your friendship immediately when you're together again. Friendship fills your need to be helpful, and this makes you happy and comfortable. Love asks you to be vulnerable, which makes you very *un*comfortable.

To Leo, your opposite sign, love is the stuff of life. Leo is the sign of romance, affection, and enjoyment. Leo people look for fun and good times to make them happy; they need strong ties with others. Leos are extravagant, magnetic, filled with fervor, and have a great sense of the dramatic. They love performing and being admired. This sign rules entertainment (such as theater, acting, games, etc.) and is aligned with the theme of finding joy and amusement.

High-spirited, hearty, and benevolent, Leos look for larger-than-life experiences, and often create them. Among Leo's best qualities are childlike enthusiasm and willingness to make the present moment radiant. They are most fulfilled by sharing their creativity, love, and generosity with intimates.

Astrologically, you as an Aquarian can benefit from adopting some of Leo's focus on heart-to-heart connections. Your tendency to seek independence at all costs can isolate you. Because you're so individualistic, you're often a loner (in your work, hobbies, interests). Showing feelings is complicated for you. You prefer to conceal what you're feeling behind a cool and friendly attitude.

Leo, on the other hand, is right out there with its emotions—very expressive and passionate. Leo has no trouble conveying joy, sorrow, needs. Leo especially needs affection and approval, and openly asks for this. Aquarius, if you let your guard down and allow yourself to be more vulnerable, you will be rewarded with true caring from others—not to mention some remarkable romantic encounters. By taking on some of Leo's in-the-moment spontaneity, you can add greater sparkle in your life on a daily basis.

In turn, Leo has much to learn from you, and at the top of this list is your equanimity in being who you are. You're not bound up in your ego the way Leo is, trying to manipulate others' attention and gain their admiration. Your confidence doesn't go up and down depending on what others are saying to you or what you think they're thinking about you. You just want the space and freedom to do your thing—and let others do theirs.

You also have far vision, and the courage to believe in the best. Your bird's-eye view of what is possible gives your imagination flight. You look to the future and don't get mired in the petty. Leo can get very stuck on itself. It exaggerates its accomplishments and represents itself as deserving of glory. In the way these things work psychologically, this makes Leo dependent. Needing others for validation, Leo's enthusiasm can burn out quickly if it isn't fanned by encouragement. You, Aquarius, believe in self-sufficiency, which makes you free to be truly original and creative.